FAMOUS JAPANESE
SWORDSMEN

FAMOUS JAPANESE
SWORDSMEN
of
The Period of Unification

日本の剣豪

William de Lange

FLOATING
WORLD
EDITIONS

First edition, 2008

Published by Floating World Editions, Inc.
26 Jack Corner Road, Warren, CT 06777
www.floatingworldeditions.com

Printed in the U.S.A.

ISBN 978-1891640-54-4

Library of Congress Cataloging-in-Publication data available

For Kinomoto Miyuki Sensei

CONTENTS

INTRODUCTION

No history of Japan's medieval era can be fully told without touching on the lives and exploits of its chief protagonists: the warriors. During the first two centuries (from the rise of the military at the end of the Heian period to the overthrow of the Kamakura Bakufu), their chief weapon was the bow and arrow; the sword seems to have played only a marginal role, for, as far as the records go, these centuries produced no great swordsmen of note. It is only later, following the overthrow of the Kamakura Bakufu, when war became incessant, that the quintessential Japanese swordsman made his debut and that we begin to see the first traces of a developing Japanese fencing tradition. Over the next two centuries, as Japan was increasingly drawn into the vortex of civil strife, these first attempts at systemization were gradually forged into distinct schools of fencing. Finally, with the drive toward unification and pacification, the many schools of fencing that survived the turmoil of the previous centuries were consolidated into a fencing tradition that came to dominate the martial arts of the Edo period.

The active history of the origin, growth, and maturation of Japanese swordsmanship, then, roughly spans the period from the beginning of the fourteenth century to the first decades of the seventeenth century—an epoch that can be divided into three distinct periods: the Two Courts period (1333–92), the Warring States period (1469–1573), and the Period of Unification (1573–1615).

This book tells the story of the two greatest swordsmen of the Period of Unification. Their names are Ono Jirōemon Tadaaki, and Yagyū Tajima no Kami Munenori. Taken together, their lives span the period during which the whole of Japan was gradually brought under central control. This period of roughly half a century was a second great turning point in Japan's medieval era. The first great turning point had come in 1333, when a disgruntled emperor sought to restore to his throne the powers it had long lost and plunged the country into civil war. From then on, generation upon generation of hapless citizens knew neither peace nor rest, hostage as they were to the whims and follies of the often ruthless and ever competing warlords. Now, after more than two centuries of almost constant strife it seemed that Japan had finally produced the kind of men who could bring the peace and prosperity for which the people were yearning. Their names were Oda Nobunaga, Toyotomi Hideyoshi, and Tokugawa Ieyasu.

It is largely to the credit of these greatest and most gifted of warlords that central authority was restored and that the torn fabric of feudal society could be repaired. It was a painful period, the crucial part of which spanned just over three decades and coincided with what is known to the Japanese as the Momoyama period. It began in 1568, when, following a short and decisive military campaign, the upstart warlord Nobunaga seized the capital. He did not appoint himself shogun. Instead, he installed at the head of the Bakufu a puppet figure, there merely to give legitimacy to his rule by proxy. That rule lasted just over a decade. By the time he was assassinated in 1582, he had brought under his control most of the Home Provinces, the provinces sur-rounding the capital and crucial to his hold on power. Nobunaga's death gave rise to Toyotomi Hideyoshi, his most gifted of generals. It was under Hideyoshi that the rest of the country, including the islands of Shikoku and Kyushu were finally subdued. Hideyoshi died a peaceful death, but the organs of state that were to secure the succession of his infant son were too weak. Its members split into two camps, one dominated by western warlords, and one dominated by eastern warlords. And it was Tokugawa Ieyasu, the leader of the eastern faction, who, in the fall of 1600 finally claimed victory in the decisive Battle of Sekigahara.

The lives of our two protagonists not only coincide with this period of civil warfare, but bore close witness to these dramatic events. Though neither of them was of sufficiently high birth to leave their mark on the larger course of Japanese feudal history, both of them played their own unique and in many ways highly illustrative roles in a number of pivotal events during this period of unrelenting warfare. Thus Ono Jirōemon Tadaaki played his own modest role in Tokugawa Ieyasu's efforts to restore order in the recently subdued Kantō. And thus Yagyū Tajima no Kami Munenori was to play his own modest role in the run-up to the epic Battle of Sekigahara.

The reader will soon find that in telling the story of these two remarkable men, much room has been given to the wider military and political events through which they lived. There are a number of reasons why this should be so, For one, to anyone interested in the history of Japanese martial arts it will be of some interest to know under what political and social conditions such military traditions were able to flourish. It was, for instance, at the cultural center of Ichijōdani castle, where the Asakura clan sought to sustain the military traditions of the Warring States period, that Tadaaki's great example Itō Ittōsai Kagehisa had enjoyed his martial training. And it was at the *dōjō* of Edo castle, Tokugawa Ieyasu's new Kantō headquarters in the wake of Hideyoshi's campaign to subdue the powerful Hōjō, that Kagehisa and Tadaaki gave a demonstration of the Ittō-ryū, the school of fencing that went back to the fourteenth century monk, Nenami Okuyama Jion. It was Ieyasu's promotion of the martial arts, too, that launched Yagyū Muneyoshi and his son Munenori on a career as shogunal fencing instructor, thereby restoring the failing fortunes of the ancient Yagyū clan and throwing into the limelight the relatively new fencing style of the Yagyū Shinkage-ryū. Ultimately, however, it was the performance of both men in the Battle of Sekigahara that decided the social status of the Ono and Yagyū clans and, more to the point, which school of fencing took pride of place at the shogunal court during the Edo period.

This broader perspective may also serve to put the contribution of these men into their proper perspective. It is in the nature of the histories of heroes that they grow more extravagant with each following generation by which they are passed on, until, in the end, their lives and exploits have become distorted beyond recognition. One of the aims of this book is to place these men firmly back in their proper context, in the place and time in which they lived and, in doing so, recapture some of the atmosphere of the period of unification—how it must have been to be a warrior in a time so rife with challenges, yet so rich in opportunities.

It is, of course, no coincidence that these remarkable two men should have lived during these trying times. Better put, it could only have been such times of upheaval and constant warfare that produced such men. It was during these times, after all, when thousands upon thousands of warriors either perished or survived simply on the strength of their martial skills and that, at the end of the day, only those with superior skills and the most effective techniques remained standing on the field of battle. It was this same process that ensured the survival of certain schools of Japanese swordsmanship and the demise of others. In this sense, it is a token of the superiority of the techniques developed by our protagonists that, in one form or other, each of the two schools of swordsmanship that they spawned have survived to this day. Japan's long feudal history has produced many swordsmen of note, but among them these two men stand out in particular, for each of them stood at the cradle of one of the schools of swordsmanship that came to dominate the art of fencing during the Edo period, the Ittō and the Yagyū Shinkage schools of fencing.

It is all the more remarkable, then, that so very little has been written about these men. Even in Japan, where so much weight has traditionally been given to pedigree and heritage, only a few serious books have been written about the origins of each school and even fewer about the lives of those who spawned them. This does not mean that there are no sources to draw on, but they remain thinly spread and the few morsels of historically reliable data that can be found have to be carefully gleaned from a wide variety and, at times, most unexpected of sources.

As has already been pointed out above, given the nature of the subject, the great majority of sources tend to indulge in hyperbole to some extent. In the same way as the famous war tales such as the *Heike monogatari* and the *Taiheiki* tend to exaggerate the number of troops that engage in the battles they describe, so the few historical sources that make mention of our heroes are riddled with inaccuracies, embellishments, or outright historical fabrications. It is the modest aim of this work to carefully filter out the hyperbole and, in doing so, represent our two protagonists and their exploits in the true light of historical fact, this in the profound belief that even their unembellished lives are sufficiently remarkable to merit our attention. If, in the telling of their tale, our heroes stand to lose some of their legendary luster, it is hoped that at the same time they gain some of that essential humanity that, in spite of all the bloodshed and horrors of the Period of Unification, never wholly left Japan, even during its darkest hours. It was that spark of humanity—that quest for an honest, simple, and quiet life—after all, that not only characterized the lives of our two heroes, but also overcame the darker forces in human nature and eventually helped restore peace to a war-torn nation.

ONO JIRŌEMON TADAAKI
(Mikogami Tenzen)

小野治郎右衛門

Eiroku 8 –Kan'ei 5
(1565–1628)

Great men often stand on the shoulders of giants, and so it was with many of the great swordsmen whose exploits coincide with the period in which Japan was gradually pacified. A classic example of the way in which the great swordsmen of the late sixteenth century built on the hard-won experience of others is Ono Jirōemon Tadaaki.

Ono Jirōemon Tadaaki was born as Mikogami Tenzen and his place of birth was Isumi, a small hamlet on the Pacific coast of the Bōsō Peninsula. Tenzen was born toward the end of the Warring States period, when the Kantō was dominated by three powerful warrior clans—the Hōjō, the Uesugi, and the Takeda. The Bōsō Peninsula, however, fell under the influence of another clan, the indomitable Satomi.

The Satomi clan originally hailed from the eponymous village on the western border of the province of Kōzuke, where they were founded by Satomi Yoshitoshi, a scion of the powerful house of Nitta. It was that clan, under the command of Nitta Yoshisada that, in the spring of 1333, had marched on Kamakura and overthrown the Hōjō. Following the reunification of the two courts toward the end of the fourteenth century, they had, like many of their allies, fallen into line and dutifully served the Ashikaga rulers. In the middle of the fifteenth century, the Satomi had been driven from their territories when their chieftain, Satomi Yoshizane, and a number of other warlords had opposed the powerful Uesugi, whose rise had lead to the death of the then *kantō kubō* Ashikaga Mochiuji. They had taken up the cause of the his two sons and ensconced themselves in Yūki castle in the neighboring province of Shimōsa. After a siege

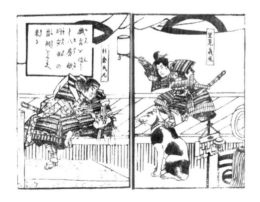

Yoshizane's son inspects the head of a fallen foe

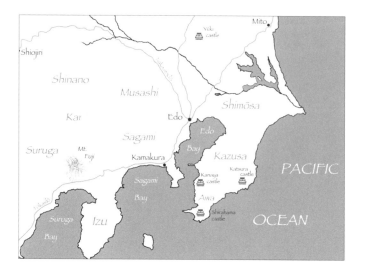

of close to half a year the castle had fallen. Only a few men, including Yoshizane, managed to escape. He fled to the tip of the Miura peninsula, where he crossed by boat over to Awa, the most southern province on the Bōsō Peninsula. There he forged an alliance with local chieftains and launched a campaign to bring the province under his control. Exploiting rivalries between the remaining clans, he quickly widened his sphere of influence on the peninsula, and within a period of no more than five years, the man who had landed on Awa's shores with little more than his sword and the clothes on his back had brought the divided province completely under his control, with the stronghold of Shirahama castle as his new seat of power.

Under Yoshizane's rule the people of Awa enjoyed greater prosperity than many other provinces during the Warring

3

Satomi Yoshizane (left), the warlord who united Awa province

States period. It was true that his task was eased by the sea's natural defense. The only border that touched other provinces consisted of semi-mountainous terrain, intersected by a few footpaths that became impassable when it rained or snowed. The chief traffic arteries all skirted the coast and were guarded by the castles of Katsura and Kanaya, and they were now under his control. It was solely to Yoshizane's credit, however, that the terrible mechanism of *gekokujō*, the law by which the lower overthrew all those above them who were weak and by which so many other provinces were plunged into abject anarchy, failed to take its toll in Awa province. Yoshizane was a true warlord in that he would launch many more campaigns in order to gain territory and thereby increase his sphere of influence, yet unlike so many other warlords he proved to be a benevolent ruler, who refrained from exploiting the population simply for the sake of his own aggrandizement. He had a keen taste for the arts, yet refrained from some of the excesses to which men in his position were prone, and always sought to find the right balance between his artistic inclinations and his martial duties. In this he was a true proponent of that medieval ideal of the cultivated warrior, like that other great warlord Kitabatake Tomonori, always in pursuit of the two inseparable moral ways, the so-called *bunbu ryōdō*, the Way of Learning and the Way of Fighting.

One of the men to benefit from Yoshizane's ascendancy was Tenzen's great grandfather, Tōchi Ōtoshi. The Tōchi clan hailed from the province of Yamato, but had been expelled from their domains at the turn of the fourteenth century when they fell foul of the Muromachi Bakufu. They had been reduced to *ochimusha*, warriors who as a result of their defeat were reliant on the hospitality and protection of others. Ōtoshi's ancestors had settled in the province of Hitachi, where they had spent a few decades in peace until they had chosen the side of Satomi Yoshizane and joined in the defense of Yūki castle.

Women retreat to the castle's upper donjon during the siege of Yūki castle

Ōtoshi had been there right from the start. He had been at Yoshizane's side during the siege of Yūki castle. He had been at his side when they had escaped across the Tone River into Musashi, and he had followed him when he resolved to cross the Uraga straits toward Awa.

In keeping with feudal tradition, Ōtoshi's share in his lord's success was equal to his display of loyalty. Yoshizane appointed him as one of ten chieftains, all men who had displayed loyalty and courage during the preceding difficult years. Like the other chieftains, Ōtoshi was allotted a modest fiefdom. His estate, with an annual rice yield of some six hundred *koku*, was situated on the outskirts of Maruyama, a village on the peninsula's eastern coast, halfway between the ports of Shirahama and Kamogawa. By the time Ōtoshi took possession of his newly acquired land, he had already taken

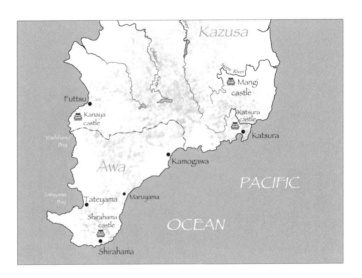

Isumi country

a wife and founded his own clan. To mark the new point of departure in his life, he had discarded the name of Tōchi and, in accordance with tradition, taken on the name of the locality in which he had settled. From now on he and his descendants went under the name of Mikogami.

Under their lord's benevolent rule the Mikogami prospered. Ōtoshi had many sons, all of whom served in the ranks of the Satomi forces. Upon his death the Mikogami estate went to his eldest son, Shōzō. Shōzō, too, occupied a high post among the Satomi forces, yet unlike his father, he held no seat on the council of chieftains. Instead, he was lieged to the house of Toki, a Mino clan, which had risen to the fore at the turn of the fifteenth century, when they helped the Satomi subdue the central regions of the Bōsō Peninsula. Their power base was Mangi castle, a formidable stronghold situated along the Isumi River some ten miles north of Katsura. Mikogami Shōzō received a plot of land along the Isumi River and served the Toki dutifully.

It was by now well into the sixteenth century. More than half a century had passed since the Ōnin War had left the capital in ruins. Much of Japan was embroiled in civil war, but thus far the Satomi hegemony had spared the dwellers on the southern part of the Bōsō Peninsula from the atrocities and hardships suffered throughout the rest of the country, Yet despite their relative isolation, it was almost inevitable that sooner or later, the peninsula's inhabitants, too, would experience at first hand what it meant to fear one's neighbors.

As with so many of the conflicts that flared up throughout Japan, the cause of the first hostilities on the southern half of the Bōsō Peninsula during the Warring States period lay not in any direct outside threat, but in unresolved internal succession disputes. For a long time the patriarchs of the Satomi had managed to keep problems among the many members of their clan in check, but all this changed in 1518, on the death of Satomi Yoshimichi, the grandson of Satomi Yoshizane. On the night before he passed away, when he already felt the shadow of death looming over him, the patriarch had passed the reins of power to his oldest son, Yoshitoyo. Many of the clan members were unhappy with the new appointment, and shortly after the old patriarch died a rift began to appear between two factions within the Satomi clan. On the one side stood the young new leader, Yoshitoyo, who had taken up residence in Inamura castle, situated at the center of the peninsula's narrowest point.

View of the Uraga Straits from Kanaya castle

The other faction was led by his uncle, Sanetaka. Sanetaka's power base was Kanaya castle, on the peninsula's west coast, just south of the port of Futtsu.

The location of both castles said a lot about the strategies that were being pursued by the two camps. As the rightful heir, Yoshitoyo was trying hard to maintain central control over his domains. Sanetaka, meanwhile, did everything in his power to undermine Yoshitoyo's rule. He had created a large seagoing force, chiefly by building on the expertise of Masaki Michitsuna, a naval expert and a descendant of the Miura clan.

Michitsuna's siding with Sanetaka was a serious blow to Yoshitoyo's prospects of maintaining central control of the southern half of the peninsula. Even more worrying news came from Yoshitoyo's spies among Sanetaka's followers, who informed him that, lately, the latter had been in secret consultation with none other than Hōjō Ujitsuna. Since the latter half of the previous century,when they had brought all

9

Hōjō Ujitsuna, the warlord who set his sights on the Bōsō Peninsula

of the Izu Peninsula under their control, the Hōjō had steadily expanded their sphere of influence northward, into the province of Sagami and toward Musashi. From what Yoshitoyo had heard, it was clear that Ujitsuna now intended to cross the Uraga Straits and invade Awa. From there he might move northward into Shimōsa so as to seize control of all of the Kantō in a two-pronged pincer movement. It was an ambitious plan, but from what Yoshitoyo knew of the Hōjō, it was not beyond their power to accomplish.

Sanetaka's collusion with the Hōjō presented Yoshitoyo with a great dilemma: was he to condone Sanetaka's scheming for the sake of unity and risk an invasion, or was he to confront his uncle and thereby inevitably disturb the peace? Yet even as he was considering the options, he realized that Sanetaka had already cast the die for him. The former's secret negotiations with the Hōjō were incontestable proof that he did not share Yoshitoyo's aim of maintaining peace on the peninsula and that, sooner or later, and with or without the help of the powerful Hōjō, he would seek to over-throw his nephew. And thus Yoshitoyo decided to rid him-self of the threat.

On July 27, 1533, he invited Sanetaka and Michitsuna to Inamura castle and had both of them murdered. The very next morning he set out with a large force toward Kanaya castle, where he knew that Sanetaka's son, Yoshitaka, as well as Michitsuna's two sons were residing. The castle fell after a short struggle, but at this point Yoshitoyo began to lose control of the plot, for while the inexperienced youths were evicted from the castle, they managed to escape unharmed, fleeing north along the coast by boat to find refuge in Tsukuroumi castle, a small stronghold on the northern out-skirts of the seaport of Futtsu. Worse still, prior to their escape, they had managed to send word to the Hōjō in Izu,

seeking Ujitsuna's assistance. The latter responded with understandable alacrity, and sent over a large force to assist Yoshitaka.

Reinforced by the Hōjō troops, Yoshitaka now marched southward, following the coast to the Fortress of Myōhon temple, situated on a high cliff overlooking Yoshihama bay, at no more than a stone's throw distance from the temple after which it was named. There he clashed with and routed Yoshitoyo's forces and captured the fortress.

Built in 1516 by Satomi Yoshimichi at the height of his power, the fortress had been a symbol of the Satomi hegemony over the southern half of the Bōsō Peninsula. To Yoshitoyo, then, the defeat at the hands of one of his own clansmen, and the help of the hated Hōjō, was all the more poignant and seemed to spell the end of the glory days of the Satomi clan. He and his men had to beat a retreat toward Takita castle, situated some five miles north of Inamura castle, but even here they were hard pressed, so that by the end

Myōhon temple

of September they were forced to flee toward Kazusa, where Yoshitoyo was taken under the protection of Mariyatsu Nobuyasu, the lord of Mariyatsu castle and a member of the Takeda clan, who were fierce enemies of the Hōjō. And it was with the latter's help that Yoshitoyo managed to raise sufficient forces to take his revenge. In April of the following year, he marched back into his former domains, determined to overthrow Yoshitaka and his accomplices.

The final showdown between the contestants came on April 6, 1534, when both forces met at Inukake, a narrow plain among the mountains surrounding Takita castle. The two armies seemed to match each other in strength, but as the day drew on and the fighting became more intense, the prospects for Yoshitoyo and his allies looked bleaker and bleaker. By noon he had lost several hundred men, and many more had fled. Then, toward the evening, as dusk began to set in, Yoshitoyo himself was slain.

It was the end of an era; a new line of the Satomi clan had seized the coveted family scepter. But now the contest was not just one between the two lines of the Satomi clan. By accepting assistance from the Hōjō, Yoshitaka had become a piece on the greater geopolitical chessboard of far more powerful and ambitious clans—clans who expected a reward for their efforts that would be more than just reciprocal. That sobering reality was borne out when, following the battle, when the severed enemy heads strewn across the battlefield were counted, Yoshitaka had Yoshitoyo's severed head cleaned, tagged, and pickled, to be sent to Odawara castle for Hōjō Ujitsuna's personal inspection.

*Inukake plain,
where Mikogami
Shōzō lost his life*

The Mikogami clan had not fought with the rightful heir in this conflict. Fate had determined that their immediate lord, Toki Tameyori, was liege to Sanetaka and his son Yoshitaka. In the Battle of Inukake, Shōzō and his eldest son, Tosa, had fought alongside the Toki, opposite the troops of Kisō Jingō, the leader of another clan of local warriors who had sided with Yoshitoyo. It was true that their side had been victorious that day, but for the Mikogami victory had come at a high cost. Casualties among their men had been high and Shōzō, the family patriarch, had laid down his life on the plain of Inukake.

Apart from having to come to terms with the death of his father, Mikogami Tosa was far from pleased with the way things had developed. He had watched with growing concern how his lord, Toki Tameyori, had grown increasingly disaffected with the policies of Yoshitaka. Tosa shared

Tameyori's concerns. Though bound in loyalty to the Satomi clan, and though he had fought on Yoshitaka's side during the battle at Inukake, Tosa had deeply regretted Sanetaka's refusal to come to terms with his nephew. He had been even more disturbed by the ease with which Sanetaka had turned toward the Hōjō, their former enemy, for help. By allowing Hōjō troops to set foot on soil that had been under Satomi control for close to a century, he had seriously compromised their autonomy. That concession had been a great blow to vassals like the Toki and the Mikogami themselves, who had come to cherish the peace and tranquility they had enjoyed under Yoshitaka's predecessors. Nor did Yoshitaka's vacillations bode well for the future stability of the region, which, in a time of war, required a strong and steady hand to keep the peace. Worse still, in return for the support they had enjoyed, the Satomi were now required to fight battles far away from home, as for instance in 1537, when a number of Yoshitaka's vassals were dispatched toward Musashi to assist Hōjō Ujitsuna in the siege of Kawagoe castle.

By then, however, it had become painfully clear that the Hōjō would never be content with the presence of just a sympathetic warlord on the peninsula. An inextricable part of their policy of expansion was the subjugation of the Bōsō Peninsula. As if to remove any lingering doubts among his enemies, in February 1538, Ujitsuna laid siege to Kasai castle, which was situated at the head of Edo Bay, and guarded the gateway into the peninsular provinces of Shimōsa, Kazusa, and Awa. And thus, in order to extricate himself from his increasingly onerous obligations toward the Hōjō and in the

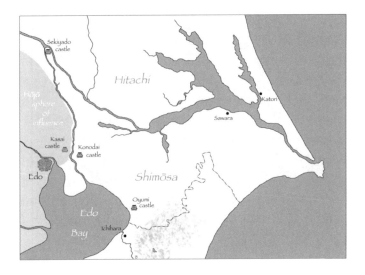

hope of maintaining some degree of autonomy over his own domains, Yoshitaka changed sides once more, this time choosing the side of Ashikaga Yoshiaki, a former monk who had returned to secular life with the vainglorious hope of restoring to the Ashikaga the authority they had once wielded in the Kantō under their powerful *kantō kubō*. Yoshiaki had already won the backing of the Mariyatsu, the Satake, and a number of other warlords in the region and installed himself in Oyumi castle, situated some fifteen miles eastward along the coast from Kasai castle. His aim was to recapture Kamakura, and it was in this endeavor that his and his ally's interests began to clash with those of a powerful and dangerous opponent in the Kantō: Hōjō Ujitsuna.

The first great showdown between the two forces came that same summer, when Ashikaga Yoshiaki, Mariyatsu Nobuyasu, and Satomi Yoshitaka assembled a huge army of some ten thousand men and began to march northward following the eastern banks of the Edo River. Their destination was Konodai castle, on the eastern bank of the Edo River, almost directly opposite Kasai castle. The latter stronghold was now the headquarters of one of Hōjō Ujitsuna's vassals. As such, it had come to mark the northeastern boundary of the Hōjō sphere of influence, and it was there, where Hōjō lines of supply were weakest, that they intended to strike the first decisive blow. Informed of his enemy's movements, Ujitsuna immediately set about raising his own army. In this he succeeded admirably well, for by the time Yoshiaki and his allies had pitched camp in the grounds of Konodai castle, Ujitsuna had arrived at Kasai castle with a force double the size, along the river's western bank.

That night, during a council among the members of Yoshiaki's camp, it was agreed that if the Hōjō forces were to initiate an attack, it would fall to the Oyumi forces, led by Yoshiaki's brother and son, to repel the initial brunt of the attack. If successful, they would then be joined by fresh and rested Satomi troops to drive the Hōjō forces back into the water and finish them off. Yoshiaki could hardly hide his resentment. Had it not been he who had rallied the rival warlords of the Bōsō Peninsula under his banner for the greater cause of ridding themselves of the looming threat of the Hōjō? During the council he held his peace, but he was determined to play his role the following day—a role, so he

17

thought, that could only be a glorious one, as he could not imagine that any Kantō warrior would dare to draw his sword against a member of the illustrious house of Ashikaga.

The day of October 7 began deceptively tranquil as the eastern sun gradually loosened itself from the sleepy landscape and put the outlines of Konodai castle in sharp relief against a crimson sky. Yet all who were gathered on the banks of the Edo River knew that soon the smooth surface of the river, glistening red in the morning sun, would be disturbed by horses and men as they rushed into the water and waded across the river to pick their enemy. Then the air would fill with the harrowing whine of bulb-arrows, the battle-cries of men, the whinnying of horses, and the clashing of steel, until, eventually, all would grow silent once more except for the cry of the ravens hovering above.

As anticipated, it was Ujitsuna who took the initiative. He ordered his men to cross the river higher upstream, where it was shallowest. They were given a warm welcome

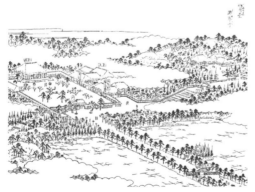

Konodai in the early Edo period

by the Oyumi forces. For several hours they managed to hold their ground, driving the Hōjō forces back into the shallows, which soon turned red with the color of spilled blood. But as the morning wore on the defending forces began to buckle under the overwhelming number of Hōjō troops, gradually giving way until those who could simply turned their backs upon the enemy and fled the scene of carnage. Aware of their untenable position, the Satomi and Mariyatsu generals urged Yoshiaki to change tactics. The best course, they suggested, was either to try and halt the enemy while they were crossing the river, or to retreat, regroup, and drive them back in a united attack.

At this crucial juncture word reached Yoshiaki that his brother and his son had been killed in the onslaught. Undaunted, they had spurred on their horses, penetrating deep into enemy lines until their horses had been shot from underneath them and both men had perished in the mayhem. Moved by their valiant deaths and irate with his commanders' lack of courage, he angrily brushed away their admonitions and, taking with him no more than two dozen mounted warriors, stormed into the breach shouting "If need be Yoshiaki will lead the assault himself and show you lot what spirit is." Those were his last words.

When warriors among the Hōjō forces noticed that none other than Ashikaga Yoshiaki had joined the melee, they scrambled forward en masse, eager to take his head in person. Yoshiaki, in spite of his rash temper, was a warrior of unsurpassed ability and no match for the common foot soldier. Lunging forward on his stallion, and wielding his three-foot

19

The reed-covered banks of Edo River

longsword, he cut his way forward, making short shrift of all who dare approach him, and causing disorder and confusion among their ranks. At length, they were even forced to execute a temporary withdrawal, creating the space and time for the exhausted general to rest his horse in the shade of a hillock along the shore and wash away the blood and gore from his drenched harness.

Spotting this scene from afar, Yokoi Kamisuke, a master archer from the Miura camp, took his strongbow and threw himself into the dense fringe of reeds that covered the river's banks. From there he waded through the cool water until he had passed well beyond the hillock and had a clear view of the unsuspecting general. Taking his time, the archer fixed his heaviest arrow to his bowstring and aimed carefully while his strong arms drew the bow that took three men to string. Even as he released his grip on the arrow and the projectile sprang away toward its target, the bowman knew he had caught his prize, that the arrow would strike home. And so it did. With a massive thud it pierced the armor on the left side of the Yoshiaki's chest, the impact causing him to reel around and reveal to the trembling archer the damage he had wrought. The iron tip of the arrow he had taken from his quiver with such steady hand only moments before now protruded from the general's back by more than three inches. For only a moment the archer beheld the arrowhead, glistening portentously like the river's crimson water, before the vital organ in which it had lodged itself gave out and the mass of armor hit the dry and hard soil in a cloud of dust.

Satomi Yoshitaka, whose men had thus far seen no serious action, stood by and did nothing. It was clear that without a rightful claimant to the governorship of the Kantō there would be little chance of capitalizing on a victory—a victory that seemed less and less likely, anyway. From what he had seen that day he knew that he would need each and every man he could rally to resist the Hōjō onslaught and hold on to his territories. And so he ordered his fresh and rested men to pack up and head back home again, while one by one the valiant warriors of the Oyumi fell until the banks of the Edo River were covered with their remains.

Mikogami Tosa had been one of many warriors who marched north with Satomi to join Ashikaga Yoshiaki's coalition forces when they pitched camp at Konodai. And neither he nor Toki Tameyori were happy with what they had seen. Yoshitaka's treacherously precipitous withdrawal had once again reminded them of his fickle nature. More

21

worrisome, the unchecked Hōjō would now certainly feel encouraged to capitalize on their victory and penetrate yet deeper into the Bōsō Peninsula.

Tosa's fears were soon borne out. Before the year was out the Hōjō had widened their sphere of influence on the peninsula as far south as Mariyatsu castle, where they installed a defected member of the Takeda clan, Mariyatsu Nobutaka, as the castle's new lord. It was a shrewd move, for it forced the other members of the Mariyatsu clan to fall back on the military aid of the Satomi. This, in turn, would inevitably lead to conflict, thus creating the perfect opportunity for the Hōjō to insinuate themselves yet further into Satomi territory. Their first real opportunity to do so came a few years later, when, between 1542 and 1543, the various members of the Mariyatsu sought to settle their differences in a contest over Sasago and Nakao castles, both of which controlled large sections of the Mariyatsu domains.

It was not only over land that the Hōjō steadily encroached upon the Satomi territories. Making good use of the seaborne troops of their allies the Miura, in the spring of 1552 a large Hōjō force under the command of Hōjō Tsunashige landed at Yoshihama Bay. It was an event laden with symbolic portent, for this was a stone's throw away form the very place where only two decades before, during the battle at the nearby fortress of the Myōhon Temple, the Satomi had first let the Hōjō intervene in their internal affairs. Ever since that first intervention, the Hōjō had fixed their covetous eyes on the provinces of the Bōsō Peninsula. For much of the next two decades their conflict with the

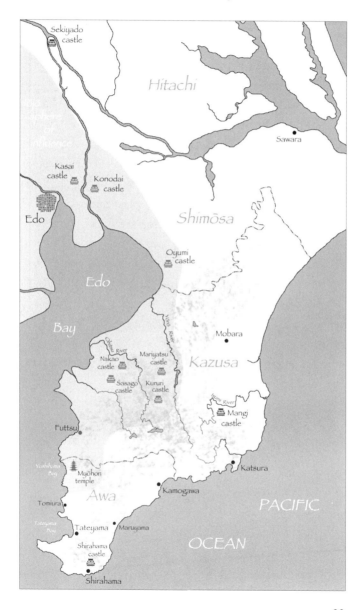

Sekiyado
castle

Hitachi

Sawara

sphere
of
influence

Kasai
castle

Konodai
castle

Edo

Shimōsa

Oyumi
castle

Edo

Mobara

Bay

Yoro River

Obitsu River

Nakao
castle

Mariyatsu
castle

Kazusa

Sasago
castle

Kururi
castle

Isumi River

Mangi
castle

Futtsu

Yoshihama Bay

Myōhon
temple

Katsura

Awa

Kamogawa

PACIFIC

Tomiura

Tateyama Bay

Tateyama

Maruyama

OCEAN

Shirahama
castle

Shirahama

other great Kantō clans in their expansion northward had kept them occupied elsewhere, but by now Tsunashige was the proud lord of Kawagoe castle, the castle that his step-brother, Ujitsuna, had captured with such ease and kept in his possession with such resilience, skill, and daring. Tsunashige, too, was keen to prove his mettle.

This he did. No sooner had he landed than he evicted the stronghold's master, who fled southward to take refuge at Kanaya castle, then still controlled by the Satomi clan. From there Tsunashige marched eastward, penetrating deep into the heart of the province. As he did so, he reduced one Satomi vassal after the other until, by the end of the next year, he had crossed the Ohitsu River, to lay siege to Kururi castle. Only years before Satomi Yoshitaka had turned the castle into his new headquarters and carried out extensive reinforcements to serve as the first line of resistance against the Hōjō threat from the north. With Tsunashige's assault from the west he now found himself fighting on two frontiers, for Mariyatsu

Kururi castle

castle, now under the control of the Hōjō, lay only three miles north from his new headquarters. For more than a year Yoshitaka held out and, in the spring of 1554, finally managed to repel the Hōjō forces from his territories with the help of the Echigo warlord Uesugi Kenshin.

The Mikogami had thus far been spared from the virulent conflict that now raged on the Bōsō Peninsula. Their estate and that of their lord, Toki Tameyori, was situated on the peninsula's eastern half, and while they themselves had taken part in much of the fighting, their lands and properties had thus far been left untouched by the conflict between the two Kantō warlords. Yet, given their allegiances and the role they had thus far played, they knew that sooner, rather than later, their extended families, their land, and their precious possessions might all be drawn into the vortex of civil war. It was a terrible threat that loomed over the not too distant horizon and a threat under which many of the smaller warrior houses collapsed.

It was with deep anxiety, then, that Tosa, the new patriarch of the Mikogami clan, learned that even his own lord, Toki Tameyori, had entered into secret negotiations with the Hōjō. He knew, for one, that already in 1542, following his victory at Konodai, Hōjō Ujitsuna had sent secret envoys to Tameyori, seeking to persuade him to change sides and avoid the kind of fate that lay in store for those who sided with the Satomi. Tameyori had turned these offers down, but the simple fact that he had received them at all had confirmed Tosa's worst fears. Moreover, it had been merely private, rather than political or even strategic concerns that

25

Tameyori had sent the envoys packing. As almost any vassal clan during Japan's feudal era, the allegiance between the Toki and the Satomi had been sealed in marriage. Tameyori's daughter was wedded to one of Yoshitaka's brothers, and it was his concern for her, rather than his respect for his overlord, that had sustained his loyalty toward the Satomi. It was no surprise to the Mikogami, then, that early in the 1560s, following the death of his daughter under mysterious circumstances, their lord was again visited by secret envoys from Hōjō Ujitsuna. Nor were they surprised to learn that this time the envoys were given a sendoff that contrasted sharply with the curt dismissal they had been given two decades earlier.

The defection of the Toki was a momentous event in the lives of the Mikogami clan. For more than a century they had faithfully served the house of Satomi. That deep bond had been forged, when Tosa's distant ancestor, Tōchi Ōtoshi, had been one of the few men who had been hand-picked by Satomi Yoshizane when he chose to escape from the besieged Yūki castle on that fateful day in April 1441. Ōtoshi had followed Yoshizane across the Tone River into Musashi, toward the Miura Peninsula. And he had followed him when a vision had told him that they should cross the Uraga Straits and rebuild their shattered lives on the Bōsō Peninsula. Over the following century, the successive chieftains of the newly founded Mikogami clan had continued to serve the Satomi, thankful for the land and rank they had been given, even after they had technically become vassals of the Toki. Now all that had changed, and their new allegiance to the hated Hōjō forced upon them by their lord was a reality hard to come to terms with.

It was in 1564 that Tosa rode out from the Mikogami estate for a second time to join the Toki and do battle at Konodai. Thus far the Toki had not openly broken with the Satomi, and they duly rallied under the Satomi banner when they and the Hōjō forces took up their positions on the banks of the Edo River. Shortly into the battle, however, it became clear that Tosa Tameyori had resolved to use his lord's treacherous methods to his own advantage, for now it was the Toki forces who stood by idly as those of Satomi Yoshitaka were being massacred before their eyes. The one sobering glimmer of hope for the Mikogami amid all this treachery was that they now seemed to be on the winning side, for in the second Battle of Konodai the Hōjō forces were again victorious. That victory, Tosa knew, would have untold consequences for him, his clan, and his estate, for he knew that the Hōjō were far from giving up on their ambitions to rule the whole of the Bōsō Peninsula.

Even in a world of sorrow and loss, there were the occasional rays of hope that pierce the morning gloom, and one was the birth to Mikogami Tosa of a son. Born in the summer of 1564, he was named Tenzen, and like his ancestors Tenzen was trained in the martial traditions of his clan from a very young age. Already at the age of ten it became clear that in his natural ability with the sword, the young boy surpassed all the other clan members. The Mikami-ryū, the school of

The young Mikogami Tenzen

fencing practiced by his clan, did not belong to any of the major schools, but wherever it may have fallen short in its technical aspects, it was amply made up for by the young Tenzen's premature insight into his opponent's movements and his extraordinary ability to adapt old and rusted techniques to fight himself out of situations for which they had never been intended. Such was his astonishing progress that already by the time he was fifteen he began to engage in *taryū shiai*, the popular contests with protagonists of other schools of fencing, and in Tenzen's day and age there was ample opportunity for such encounters.

The Warring States period was now at its zenith. There was not a province untouched by internal strife, hardly a corner of Japan that was not mobilized, and not a town that was not awash with soldiers. As they passed through villages and hamlets on their way from one scene of battle to the other, the troops put an immense burden on the hapless populace, who had to feed and often keep the soldiers with the little

28

means they had. Capitalizing on the general state of lawless-ness, large bands of heavily armed bandits, many of them dis-affected samurai or *ashigaru* who had gone without payment for too long, pillaged and raped their way through a society that was already deeply scarred by the ravishes of internecine warfare. It took men of some resolve, then, to venture outside the relative safety of their lord's domain, and even more so engage on a journey in active pursuit of some-one with whom to engage in a duel. It seemed that Tenzen belonged to this group of brave men. By the time he had reached the age of seventeen, he had already duelled with most of the swordsmen of note on the Bōsō Peninsula.

There were few other schools of fencing on the Bōsō Peninsula on which an aspiring swordsman could draw for inspiration. One was the Tachimi-ryū, a school founded dur-ing the Muromachi period by Tachimi Mikyō. His descen-dants had settled in Sakura, where they had founded a clan and propagated Mikyō's style of fencing. Sakura lay in the province of Shimōsa, but the teachings of the Tachimi school had soon spread beyond its borders. Among the swordsmen with whom Tenzen practiced, some had been on *musha shugyō* and traveled down south, to the Izu peninsula for instance, where they had come into contact with practi-tioners of the Tamiya-ryū, or farther still, to the distant island of Kyūshu, the home of the exotic Sekiguchi and Shigen-ryū. Most, however, had learned their skills closer to home, at the famous Katori and Kashima shrines in the vil-lages of Sawara and Kashima, the birthplaces of the Katori and Kashima Shintō schools of fencing.

*Saitō Denkibō, disciple of
Tsukahara Bokuden and
founder of the Ten-ryū*

All of these men were good swordsmen, but their skills
paled in significance when compared to the kind of fencing
practiced by any of the big names of the time, men such as
Ogasawara Nagaharu, an exponent of the great Kamiizumi
Nobutsuna's Shinkage-ryū. Men such as Okuyama Kyūgasai
Kimishige, who had also studied fencing under Nobutsuna,
but was known for his Okuyama style of fencing. Or the
fearsome Saitō Denkibō Katsuhide, a disciple of Tsukahara
Bokuden and founder of the Ten-ryū. Like their former mas-
ters, these illustrious swordsmen freely traveled the length
and breadth of the country on their *musha shugyō*, seeking to
deepen their understanding of their craft through meditation and honing it in contests with men of their own standing. Thus far Tenzen had not had the opportunity to engage
with swordsmen of such repute. He would have to wait
another decade before that opportunity would present itself.

The world in which Tenzen grew up was one of constant strife and turmoil. The Hōjō had not forgotten their invasion of the early fifties and their failure to reduce Kururi castle. For ten years Satomi Yoshitaka had managed to hold on to the castle and keep the enemy at bay. Following the second Battle at Konodai, the Hōjō had launched another campaign to capture the Bōsō Peninsula. Again they had penetrated deep into the peninsula, right up to the borders of the Satomi domains. To guard their newly acquired territories, they built a fortress on the slopes of Mount Mifune, just south of Kimitsu, a small port on the peninsula's west coast. At one stage they even captured Kururi castle, but by 1567 the Satomi had recovered and driven their foes back toward Mifune. There, on a desolate plain in the shade of the fortress the two forces engaged in a battle for supremacy.

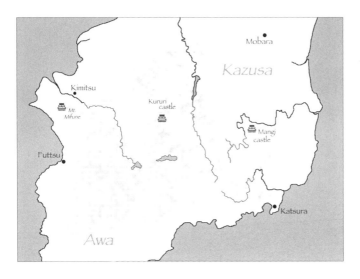

The Battle of Mount Mifune ended in an unqualified victory for the Satomi and their allies. Having suffered close to two-and-a-half thousand casualties, the Hōjō forces once again withdrew from the Bōsō Peninsula.

Nominally, the contest for the peninsula was between the Hōjō and the Satomi, but on the field of battle the real fighting was done by smaller, local clans. They were the clans that were either forced to protect their lord's interests, or chose to protect their own. Among them were clans such as the Fujizawa, who hailed from the province of Kōzuke, like the Satomi. During the previous decade it had resisted Takeda Shingen's expansion into their province. Following the fall of Minowa castle, a number of its members had gone over to the Hōjō and had been fighting battles on their behalf ever since. Another clan that hailed from Kōzuke were the Tanaka. And it had been these two clans who had been ordered by Hōjō Ujimasa, the new Hōjō chieftain, to build the fortifications on Mount Mifune.

Hōjō Ujimasa, the new leader of the Hōjō clan

Ōtaki castle, seat of power of Masaki Tokishige

In their fight for supremacy on the peninsula the Fujizawa and the Tanaka were pitted against a number of formidable enemies, local clans like the Masaki, whose ancestors had been driven from the Miura peninsula by the Hōjō at the turn of the fifteenth century. They had settled in the vicinity of Ōtaki, a few miles westward along the Isumi River from the Mikogami estate. At that time the area around Ōtaki was still controlled by a branch of the Mariyatsu, who had built a castle by the same name on the western bank of the Isumi River. But in 1544, when the Mariyatsu became embroiled in an internal family feud, the Masaki chieftain, Masaki Tokishige, the son of the naval expert Masaki Michitsuna, and a warrior famed for his ability with the *yari*, had jumped into the resulting power vacuum and made Ōtaki castle his own. Not long afterward, his brother, Tokitada, did the same with Katsuura castle, which controlled the eponymous port on the peninsula's east coast. In 1567 both of them fought hard during the Battle of Mifune, and it was largely to their credit that the huge Hōjō force had been driven from the peninsula.

As an indigenous clan of the Bōsō Peninsula the Toki, too, had an interest in the outcome of the battle at Mifune, but since their own territories were not directly at stake, they had stood back and let the other local clans do the fighting. Repeatedly the outermost reaches of the Hōjō sphere of influence had spread southward on the peninsula, right up to the borders of the Toki domains, but never yet had any part of the Toki territories become the venue of a major battle between the Hōjō and the Satomi.

All this changed dramatically following the fall of Sekiyado castle. Situated in the fork of the Tone and Edo rivers, the castle was considered by many to be impenetrable. Despite their victories at Konodai, the Hōjō had thus far failed to overcome this obstacle in their expansion eastward. It had remained a thorn in their side, doing much, too, to deflate their efforts to win the peninsula by proxy. Twice before, first in 1565, then in 1568, the Hōjō had tried to bring the castle to heel, and twice before they had failed. But, in 1574, the inevitable happened when Ujimasa signed a pact with his arch enemy Takeda Shingen and, his hands now free, raised a huge force to subdue the castle once and for all.

Within a year the Hōjō forces were back on the peninsula, capturing one stronghold after another and forcing local chieftains either to submit to their rule or to commit suicide. By the spring of 1575 Mobara and Ichinomiya were under their control and Hōjō troops were stationed along the northern bank of the Isumi River, the natural northern

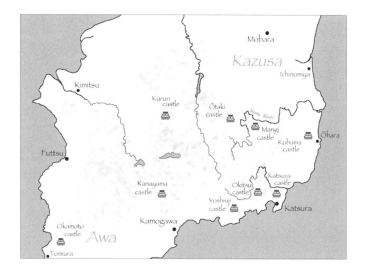

line of defense of the Toki domains. After a decade of subterfuge and prevarication, Toki Tameyori was forced to
show his hand. The Hōjō were getting ready to launch an
assault on the Satomi domains. His own lay in their way, and
he knew that they would cross them sooner or later, with or
without his help. The Satomi, of course, would never brook
his defection. Yet their new leader, Yoshihiro, was the son
of Tameyori's daughter. His only hope, then, was that
Yoshihiro would buckle at a straight-out offensive against
his maternal grandfather, and instead concentrate on keeping the Hōjō at bay. Finally, in the summer of 1575, when he
no longer could sustain the pretence, Tameyori allowed the
Hōjō troops to cross the Isumi River and enter his domains.

As Tameyori had hoped, the response from Kururi castle
was ambiguous. Hearing of the defection of the Toki, the

*The tranquil
waters of
Isumi River*

new Satomi patriarch was rightfully incensed, but his close family ties to the Toki apparently got the better of him, for instead of riding out himself, Yoshihiro ordered the Masaki to cross the Isumi River from the east and attack Mangi castle. Yet the constant fighting on behalf of the Satomi had seriously weakened the fighting strength of the Masaki, who had thrown close to eight thousand men into the Battle of Mifune, and were now reduced to less than half.

The Toki, by contrast, had hugely benefited from their passive stance over the previous years. They could not put as many men into the field, but those who did fight were well fed and motivated, and with the help of the Hōjō, they were able to drive the Masaki back across the Isumi River. No further initiatives were taken by the Satomi over the following years, too preoccupied as they were with keeping the Hōjō outside the borders of their own domains. In 1577 the two camps reached a tentative truce, but the previous decades had taken their toll, for one year later Satomi

Yoshihiro passed away at the age of forty-seven, drained and exhausted by the constant fighting.

For the Mikogami clan the truce came as a great relief. The border of their estate ran right along the eastern bank of the Isumi River, causing it to coincide with the new frontier and leaving them to be the first to feel the tensions it caused. Tenzen had been only eleven years old when the Masaki had crossed the river and launched their assault on Mangi castle. And though he had been too young to take part in any direct fighting, he had played his part in the defense of their domains, carrying water and food to his father and the other Toki warriors who had ensconced themselves in makeshift battlements along the riverbank. During the lull in the fighting over the next few years he and his family members had trained hard to enhance their fighting skills. He had soon outshone his sparring partners, and the more he mastered the art of fencing, the more he craved an encounter with the great men that featured in the tales

Mangi castle, seat of power of the Toki clan

37

that he had heard on his visits to the local tavern. Thus far Tenzen had not had the opportunity to engage with a warrior of such repute, but this changed in the summer of 1583, when a swordsman by the name of Itō Ittōsai Kagehisa took up lodgings in a hostel in the town of Isumi and let it be known that he was eager to engage in a *taryū shiai*.

In line with the martial conventions of the day, Kagehisa had put up a notice on the local news board, challenging any swordsman in the vicinity to come forward and confront him in man-to-man combat. Having grown up in a relatively isolated part of the country Tenzen knew only little about the man who was now occupied one of the upper rooms of the local hostel, but the few rumors that he had picked up had made it more than clear that this was the man to beat if he were to make a name for himself as a master swordsman.

Tenzen knew that Itō Ittōsai Kagehisa was not the average run-of-the-mill swordsman. Many believed that he was the most accomplished swordsman of his generation, and among all the swordsmen who could be found on the road in Tenzen's time, there were only few who could boast that they had had the temerity to engage the man in a duel. Those who had done so had invariably lost, and many among them had, at some stage or other, been among his large following of *deshi*, or disciples. Yet despite his fame, much of Kagehisa's life and background remained covered in a veil of secrecy. Unlike the extrovert Tsukahara Bokuden, who was still alive when Tenzen was born, and whose ostentatious

Itō Ittōsai Kagehisa, most accomplished swordsman of his generation

musha shugyō were already the stuff of legends, Kagehisa usually traveled alone and he never actively sought the limelight, even though his long and eventful life gave him ample occasion to do so. Taking on the likes of Ittōsai was an immense risk, but for a budding swordsman like Tenzen the opportunity to measure himself against a master swordsman was a chance he could not let go.

Thus it was, that on a cool November morning in 1583, the two swordsmen faced each other in the garden of the hostel. Tenzen's had dressed himself in his most splendid garments and had brought along an array of arms. To his surprise, however, his antagonist was very modestly dressed, wearing no more than a dusty *hakama* and a thin cotton upper garment, both faded and worn by a life on the road. His amazement grew when, having agreed to use practice swords, the senior swordsman refrained from using the so-called *bokken*, a weapon crafted from tropical hardwood for the aim of man-to-man practice. Instead, he simply walked to a corner of the yard to pick up a length of discarded wood, weighed it in his hands and, seemingly lost in his own thoughts, moved back to the center of the yard to take up his position opposite the young local swordsman. Seeing his chance clear, the audacious Tenzen immediately charged, but the moment he came within reach of Kagehisa's piece of wood, uttering a *kiai* from the depths of his stomach as he brought down his weapon, he felt an electrifying surge run through the lower end of his left arm. Striking upward with the course piece of wood, Kagehisa had landed a crushing upward blow on Tenzen's left wrist, paralyzing the hand's grip on his *bokken*, and causing it to tumble over the master's head and land with a thud at the other end of the yard. Nursing the aching wrist the young swordsman immediately bowed to recognize his superior, but the latter merely frowned, placed the piece of wood back from where he had taken it, and withdrew into the hostel.

The young and ambitious swordsman had been utterly defeated. Yet amid the disappointment and anger of defeat Tenzen knew that he had had a life-changing experience. For a brief and fleeting moment he had tasted at a level of swordsmanship that surpassed anything he had seen or practiced before. He needed to know the source of such knowledge, and thus he once more mustered his courage and followed Kagehisa into the hostel. To Tenzen's amazement Kagehisa seemed pleased, almost grateful for his attention and invited the young man to join him for a simple lunch over which he would tell him of the events that had led him to the remote part of the country. As they sat down to a lunch of pickles and a bowl of rice the young warrior listened with relish as the old man recounted the story of his life.

Kagehisa did not recall the exact year of his birth, but he knew that he was born sometime during the Tenbun era (1532–54). He hailed from Itō, a small port on the eastern shore of Izu Peninsula. There, he had been raised as a fisherman and his original name was Maebara Yagorō. As a young lad he had often joined his father when he sailed over to Ōshima island, an experience that had kindled in him the eagerness to travel. His greatest ambition, however, was to be a swordsman. From a young age he had pursued the art of fencing, albeit without a master. Before he reached the age of twenty he had fought a number of duels, winning all of them, until he had met with a certain Toda Ippō, at whose hands he was utterly defeated. It was with a melancholy glance at Tenzen that Kagehisa recalled how the latter had taken pity on him, written a letter of recommendation, and urged him to travel down to Echizen and enter the service of the Asakura clan, with whom the Toda warriors had long entertained close links.

Among the many warrior clans that inhabited the Japanese isles the Asakura clan was one of the most colorful. Their first great leader during the Warring States period was Asakura Takakage, who, during the middle of the fifteenth century, had fought and won a string of military campaigns to strengthen his position in Echizen. At the outbreak of the Ōnin War he and his men had been in the front lines.

Already at that time the Asakura warriors were renowned
for their intelligence and military prowess, and the leaders of
both the Eastern and Western armies had wanted him
among their ranks. Bound in loyalty to the Shiba clan, he had
at first fought on the side of his overlord Shiba Yoshikado,
the constable of Echizen, who had joined the Western
Army. But in 1471, when fighting had reached a critical
point, he returned home and declared himself a servant of
the shogun. The move had won him the position of constable of Echizen, and over the following years he continued to
reinforce his position. He built a huge castle along the
Ichijōdani River, some ten miles southeast of Fukui, and
proceeded to impose heavy taxes on the region's manorial
lords. With these he financed his campaigns of expansion,
distributing among his vassals the possessions of the manor-

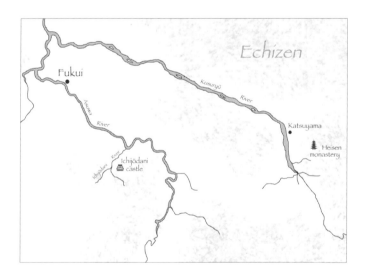

The beautiful valley of Ichijōdani

ial lords and monasteries of the regions he had conquered. In doing so, Takakage became one of the first great warlords of the Warring States period.

The Asakura leaders were ruthless, yet they were not barbarians. Takakage, too, was a great believer in *bunbu ryōdō*, the dual way of martial and civil accomplishments. Trying to capture some of the cultural mood of the capital he laid out within the precincts of Ichijōdani castle vast and beautiful gardens in the Muromachi style. Set among these were a large number of buildings: living quarters, a meeting hall, and a tea house, as well as a large library. Of course there were also the obligatory *dōjō*, for his warriors to practice the arts of spear fighting and fencing, for the Asakura were first and foremost warriors who lived and sustained their power by adhering to the clan's warrior code. Living in a period of civil war, that code was deeply informed by the immutable law of *gekokujō*. It was a cynical and utterly ruthless mechanism, an unwritten law, which in its ultimate conclusion

43

came dangerously close to total anarchy. Yet, in its own, almost perverse way, it was also a law that allowed merit to take precedent over any other distinction by which society was organized, be it rank, status, or pedigree. It was with this in mind that, during the last year of his reign, the pragmatic Takakage compiled the *Asakura Takakage jūshichikajō*, a compendium of house rules by which he expected his descendants to conduct their affairs. Some of the most striking among these were the injunctions that:

- In the Asakura clan appointments should not be given to elders. Advisers are to be recommended on the basis of ability and loyalty.
- Do not appoint people without ability to lands or posts just because they have served the Asakura for more than one generation.
- Heirloom swords and daggers and the like should not to be unduly coveted, for even if one were to possess a longsword worth ten thousand pieces one could not overcome a hundred spears worth a hundred pieces each.
- Three times a year one should send honest and capable retainers to travel around the province and inquire into the views of people of all classes in order to remedy errors of government.
- On occasions when one receives direct reports, do not even in the slightest contort the rights and wrongs of a case. If reports concerning officials who line their own pockets or the like happen to come to your knowledge, be firm in imposing a commensurate sentence.

It was this remarkably progressive emphasis on merit and justice that attracted ambitious and able warriors by the hundreds from far afield to serve the Asakura over the following century. Takakage in his time may not have thought highly of swords and daggers, but many of these men were famous swordsmen, like, for instance, the warriors of the Toda clan. One of them was a man by the name of Nagaie, a fierce warrior who had studied the art of fencing under none other than Chūjō Nagahide, the one-time pupil of the great Nenami Jion. Toda Nagaie had used Nagahide's teachings of the Chūjō-ryū to develop his own style of fencing, which he had branded the Toda-ryū. Nagaie's descendants must have inherited his qualities for they continued to serve the Asakura clan.

By the time the young Maebara Yagorō arrived at Ichijōdani castle the Asakura chieftaincy was in its eleventh generation. Asakura Yoshikage was now the lord of the castle, and like his famous ancestor Yoshikage was a dedicated

Former samurai
dwellings at
Ichijōdani castle

patron of the arts, both martial and civil. His and his ancestor's patronage had created a climate in which the martial arts prospered as never before.

Pride of place in the martial traditions of the Asakura clan was taken by the Toda school of fencing, although its teaching remained under the firm control of the Toda clan. Their ancient tradition had been handed down from Toda Nagaie to his son Kageie, who in turn had passed it down to his sons Kagemasa and Seigen. Kagemasa was an accomplished swordsman, but it was Seigen who was born with a natural gift for the art of fencing and surpassed both his brother and his father. Seigen, by this time was already in his forties, and as the chief propagator of the Toda-ryū, he had under his wing a great number of *deshi*, aspiring swordsmen, who, like the young Yagorō, had flocked to Ichijōdani castle in the hope of improving their skills. All of these men came from clans with their own style of fencing, yet all of them realized that the Toda-ryū, with its history that went back all the way

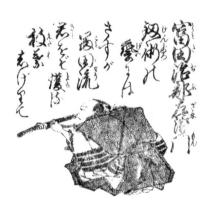

Toda Kagemasa, grandson of Toda Nagaie, the pupil of Chūjō Nagahide

46

Toda Seigen, born with a natural gift for the art of fencing

to the great Nenami, was superior. Among the many *deshi* were men such as Yamazaki Rokusaemon, whose clan hailed from the neighboring province of Ōmi, and whose ancestors had served the Asakura since the turn of the fifteenth century. He showed such ability in the techniques of the Toda school that he became Seigen's star *deshi*, and at length had been fully adopted into the clan's household. He married Kagemasa's daughter and received the name of Shigemasa. Men like Toda Shigemasa occupied far too lofty a position to give much notice to the young Yagorō, but among the many warriors who fought for the Asakura clan there were others, men with the same humble background as Yagorō, and it was one of them, a man by the name of Kanemaki Jisai, who, over the next few years, came to play an important role in the budding swordsman's life.

Kanemaki Jisai's background was perhaps even more obscure than that of Yagorō, but he was a man of exceptional talent, whose love of swordsmanship was only

47

Kanemaki Jisai at his studies

matched by his love of books. He had arrived at Ichijōdani several years before Yagorō did, and his talent and diligence were spotted by Toda Kagemasa, who made him one of his three star pupils. It must have been their common background that brought the two young men together, for not long after Yagorō's arrival Jisai took the young swordsman under his wing and taught him what he had learned from the Toda brothers. In keeping with the Asakura tradition, both young swordsmen not only spent many a day in the *dōjō* in practice, but also spent a lot of time in the Asakura library in the pursuit of learning. Here, too, it was Jisai whose talents surpassed that of his fellow pupils. He had made a serious study of the Musō school and its history and recorded his findings in the *Musō kenshin hōshō*, the first tract on this ancient school of fencing, written under his alias of Toda Ittōsai. Yagorō, of course, also studied Jisai's work, and it was out of respect for his friend's learning that he adopted the second part of his pen name as his own.

Thus it was that, over the course of a decade, the young man acquired his first thorough grounding in an art of swordsmanship that went all the way back to the latter days of the Two Courts period, when a young itinerant monk by the name of Nenami Jion had set his mind on avenging his murdered father. Eventually Yagorō's talents, too, were recognized by the Toda clan, from which he received his third name of Kagehisa. Furnished with a new second and third name, the swordsmen who had begun his life as a humble fisherman from the port of Itō, from now on went by the name of Itō Ittōsai Kagehisa.

Kagehisa's studies were greatly encouraged by Asakura Yoshikage. As a self-proclaimed patron of the arts he left no stone unturned to further the intellectual development of his retainers and thereby bolster the prosperity of his domains. These aspirations often brought the warlord to Kyoto, where he frequented tea ceremonies at the mansions of high nobles. He even entertained close connections

Asakura Yoshikage,
patron of the arts

49

with the shogun Ashikaga Yoshiaki, from whom he had received the first character of his given name. And it was Yoshikage's connections with the shogunal house that were to set in motion a sequence of events that would lead to the destruction of the Asakura clan.

Asakura Yoshikage's friendship with the shogun went back to 1565. In that year the treacherous Yamato warlord Matsunaga Hisahide had assassinated Yoshiaki's older brother and shogun, Yoshiteru, together with his wife and mother. Yoshikage had taken Yoshiaki in protection and given him refuge at Ichijōdani castle. Yet the warlord's reluctance to march on the capital and install the rightful heir had driven Yoshiaki in the hands of Oda Nobunaga, who had gratefully seized the opportunity to further his own political aspirations. In 1568 he had seized the capital and installed Yoshiaki as his puppet ruler. The latter, of course,

Ashikaga Yoshiaki, brother
of the murdered shogun

Oda Nobunaga, the ambitious warlord who used Yoshiaki to further his own political aims

soon tired of his symbolic and empty role; he craved the kind of power his ancestors had once wielded, and within a year he began to send secret missives to powerful warlords who might help him realize that ambition and crush Nobunaga. The latter responded by sending his own missives, inviting the warlords to attend a meeting where he intended to discuss the affairs of state. Yoshikage received both missives with good grace, yet refrained from lifting a finger in support of either party. For Nobunaga it was the proof he needed.

At the end of May 1570, Nobunaga left Kyoto at the head of some thirty thousand men. He headed for the province of Wakasa, ostensibly to punish another warlord who had failed to attend the meeting. When, however, had he reached Imazu, he continued northward, to Tsuruga. There he began to lay siege of castles controlled by Asakura vassals, first Tezutsuyama, and then Kanagasaki, the famous stronghold that had played such a pivotal role in the fighting during the

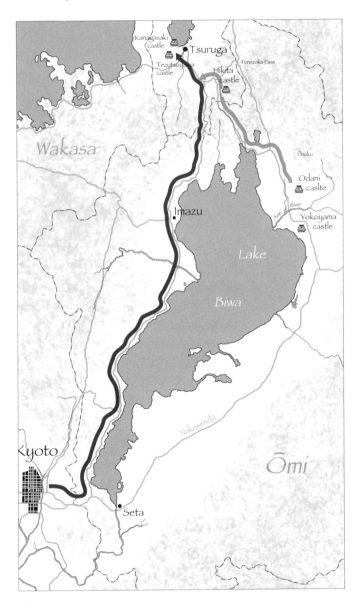

Two Courts period. This time the castle fell without a fight. Nobunaga was now poised to march on Fukui and Ichijōdani, but at this crucial moment things turned against him. To make his campaign into a success he relied on the cooperation of surrounding warlords. One of them was Asai Nagamasa, the lord of Odani castle, the headquarters from which he controlled the province of Ōmi. Nagamasa had married Nobunaga's sister and had been among those who had attended Nobunaga's council, giving Nobunaga good reason to believe he was a reliable ally. In secret, however, the Asai were in collusion with the Asakura, for when Nobunaga reached Echizen, Nagamasa cut off his retreat and attacked his rear flank. Taken by surprise, Nobunaga was forced to make a hasty retreat toward Kyoto, straight through the Asai territories. It was chiefly through the valor and tactical skill of the commander of the rear guard, Toyotomi Hideyoshi, that, on the last day of the month, the bulk of his forced safely reached the capital's outskirts.

Nobunaga was now even more determined to crush his antagonists in Ōmi and Echizen, and he wasted no time in achieving that aim. In the summer of that same year he called in the help of Tokugawa Ieyasu, the powerful warlord of Mikawa province. Ieyasu responded and on July, 21 he and some five thousand of his men joined Nobunaga's forces, which had laid siege of Yokoyama castle, on the southern banks of the Ane River only a few miles south of the Asai stronghold of Odani castle. They were met from the other side by the combined forces of the Asai and the Asakura clans, some eighteen thousand warriors in all.

Thus far Ittōsai Kagehisa had seen little action. He and his fellow swordsmen had been present when the Asakura forces helped the Asai drive Nobunaga out of Ōmi, but their swords had stayed in their scabbards. Flintlock muskets, know in Japan as *teppō*, or "iron bars," had long since made their debut on the field of battle. Nobunaga had been one of the first warlords to capitalize on their effectiveness in open confrontations; their use had enabled his troops to retreat behind a hail of bullets. Now, as the two forces took positions on opposite sides of the Ane River, it soon became clear that at least in this battle, he and his fellow swordsmen need not fear the might of the *teppō*, since the troops that faced them across the river were those of Tokugawa Ieyasu. Nobunaga's forces were stationed further eastward along the river. Numerically, too, they seemed to hold the advantage,

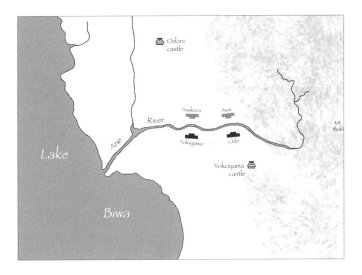

for while the total number of the opposing forces approached thirty thousand, the majority were facing those of the Asai upriver. The only thing that worried the warriors was the absence of their lord, Yoshikage, who had remained behind at Ichijōdani castle. Rumors had it that he had become infatuated with a young boy. He had entrusted the command of his troops to his relative Asakura Kagetake.

Intense fighting eventually erupted in the early hours of July 28, when two of Ieyasu's divisions crossed the Ane River and engaged the Asakura forces. Kagehisa and the other swordsmen fought hard in the humid heat of that early summer day. They brought all their fighting skill and expertise to bear on their opponents. And they fought valiantly—so valiantly, indeed, that even their enemies had to concede. The *Nobunaga-ki*, written by the Edo historian Oze Hoan, and based on the accounts of Nobunaga's close vassal Ōta Ushikazu, describes how:

> In the thick of the fight, a single mounted warrior from among the Asakura ranks by the name of Magara Jurōzaemon spurred on his horse, and, wielding around a five-foot longsword as if it were the wheel of a water mill, drove straight into the middle of the enemy ranks and called out "those who have the stomach come forward and fight me in hand to hand combat."

His challenge was met by two warriors from among the Tokugawa ranks, who stepped forward and announced their names and pedigree as custom required. They were the spearmen Sakisaka Shikebe and Gorōjirō, brothers who

The Battle of Anegawa, which determined the fate of the house of Asakura

belonged to the battalion of Sakai Tadatsugu. As they confronted and sized each other up, all fighting around them ceased, as the warriors of both camps watched with bated breath how the duel would end. One of the two lancers charged, thrusting his lance toward the mounted warrior, but the latter parried it with such force that the tip of the lance broke off. The lancer, who lost his balance and lunged forward, was almost decapitated by the trajectory of the sword, which went straight through the guards of his helmet. At this, his brother lancer and a number of his retainers crowded in on the horseman and collectively thrust their weapons at Jurōzaemon breast. Wounded and drained of his strength the mounted warrior dropped his head and, feeling his life ebbing away, spoke his last heroic words: "take my head and make it one of your feats."

In seemed that day that the duel between the lone swordsman and his waylayers epitomized the state of affairs, for in spite of their valor Kagehisa and his fellow warriors were fighting a losing battle. Their commander Asakura Kagetake was an able general, but came nowhere close to the caliber of Tokugawa Ieyasu, who in spite of his numerically inferior position, managed to keep up pressure on the Asakura troops. Nobunaga, who had started out from a superior position, was faring less well. In spite of their inferior number the Asai had launched a fierce attack on his troops. They had penetrated deep into the Nobunaga ranks, crushing one phalanx after another until only two out of thirteen held its position. His rescue came from a number of *atozume*, reserve battalions, which had been posted in the vicinity of Yokoyama castle to keep its occupants in check. They were now employed to deliver a crushing blow on the left and right flanks of the Asai battalions. It was a decisive moment. Feeling themselves squeezed from all sides, the Asai forces began to retreat toward the safety of Odani castle, leaving those of the Asakura painfully exposed. At this the Asakura, too, began to retreat, yielding to their opponents a victory that had almost been theirs. Had they been led by a more forceful commander they would assuredly have won the day, but neither Kagetake, nor any of the other commanders under which they served that day had the kind of boldness or grit of the great Kantō warlords.

Though they had survived the defeat at Ane River, the Asakura and the Asai never fully recovered from its effects. Nobunaga failed to reduce Odani castle, but he had captured the nearby stronghold of Yokoyama, which provided him with a lasting foothold in the region. For a while he was distracted by his old arch enemy Takeda Shingen. But when, in the spring of 1573, the latter died of old age, Nobunaga finally had his hands free to deal with the Asai and Asakura.

In the same year, on August 8, Nobunaga returned to Yokoyama castle with a force of thirty thousand troops to crush the Ōmi and Echizen resistance. Again Asakura Yoshikage raised troops to help the besieged Asai, but this time a number of his chief vassals refused to join him on the grounds that their armies were too exhausted by the previous campaigns. With the help of his vassal Yamazaki Yoshiie he finally raised a force of some twenty thousand men, at the head of which he marched on Odani castle. There followed no immediate clash and within a week both armies had entrenched themselves in a number of fortifications amid the mountainous terrain in the castle's vicinity. On August 12, the region was hit by a fierce typhoon and as the guards sought shelter under makeshift roofs, their armor drenched and steaming in the sudden cool, it seemed to many of the warriors that their leaders had chosen a very inauspicious moment to settle their differences.

Nobunaga thought otherwise. Knowing that his opponents would be hiding from the rain he took some thousand foot soldiers and, under the cover of thick sheets of driving rain attacked Ōzuku, a makeshift hill fortress the Asakura had erected just north of Odani castle. Its force of five hundred men was utterly taken by surprise and could do little else than surrender. The same happened with another fortress manned by *sōhei* from the Heisen monastery. The

monastery, situated some ten miles east from Ichijōdani castle, belonged to the Tendai, a sect that supported the
Asakura in its fight against central control.

Hearing of the fall of the two strongholds, Yoshikage lost
his nerve. That same night he ordered his troops to retreat
along the Hokkoku Kaidō, hoping to reach the safety of
Hikita castle, on the safe side of the Nosaka Mountains. Yet
even before they had reached the Tonezaka pass Nobunaga
caught up with them, delivering a withering attack on their
rear flank. It was a devastating blow in which close to three
thousand of Asakura's men were killed. Thirty-eight of them
were commanders, among them two of Yoshikage's close
relatives, as well as Yamazaki Yoshiie, the vassal who had
helped raise a force that had proved incapable of withstand-
ing Nobunaga's modern army.

Yoshikage now abandoned all intentions of confronting
his enemy in the field and headed straight home for
Ichijōdani castle. Only a few days later, on August 18,

*Yamazaki Yoshiie
(left) offers his life
for a lost cause*

Nobunaga's troops, too, reached the Ichijō valley and began to burn down all the buildings in the vicinity. By now most of Yoshikage's former vassals had been killed in action. The remainder, sensing that his end was near, had deserted him, and it seemed that there was no escaping Nobunaga's wrath. Only Asakura Kageaki, the lord of Iyama castle in Ōno, came to the besieged warlord's aid. Earlier he had refused to contribute his troops for reasons of fatigue, but now he suggested that Yoshikage come to Ōno, where he could stay at the Kenshō monastery, on the precincts of the castle. From there they could always retreat into the mountains and rely on the help of the *sōhei* of the nearby Heisen monastery.

With no other recourse, Yoshikage had his horse readied and, taking with him a small group of retainers, fled northward to Ōno and what he hoped would be the safety of the Kenshō monastery. Yet even here he did not find safety. Already the abbot of the Heisen monastery had signed a pact with Nobunaga's general Toyotomi Hideyoshi. If they were to assist in the drive toward unification, they would be allowed to hold on to their lands and properties in Echizen. Kageaki, too, was in collusion with Hideyoshi, having agreed to deliver Yoshikage into his hands on similar conditions. Shortly after Yoshikage and his retinue had arrived at the Kenshō monastery they were surrounded by Kageaki's men. All, except the warlord, were put to death. Yoshikage was allowed to retreat into the monastery's inner sanctum where, at the age of forty-one, he disemboweled himself. His body was cremated and interred at the local cemetery, but his head was sent to Nobunaga for inspection.

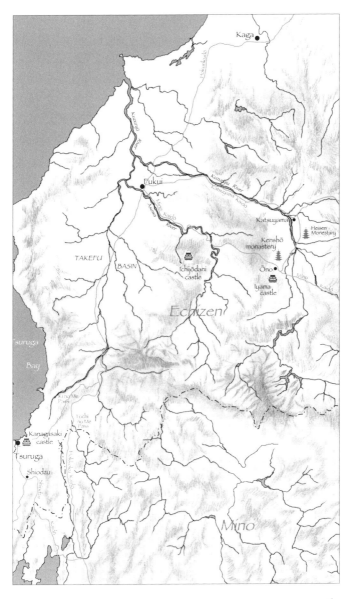

All of the great warriors of the house of Asakura were now dead, and only few of the men Kagehisa had known were still alive. Among them were his close friends Kanemaki Jisai, and Toda Seigen's star *deshi*, Toda Shigemasa. Had they not been dismissed by Yoshikage when he left for Ōno, all three of them would assuredly have died at the hands of Kageaki's henchmen. On August 19, one day before Nobunaga entered Ichijōdani castle, they had set off eastward, along the Mino Kaidō. That same day they had crossed the Aburazaka pass and reached the safety of Mino province. Eventually, however, they had gone their own separate ways.

For the next ten years Kagehisa had led the life of a *rōnin*, a masterless samurai, traveling from one province to another, at times in pursuit of employment, at times in pursuit of a duel, and it was one of those travels that had now brought the seasoned warrior to the province of Kazusa and the small hamlet of Isumi. Given the demise of the house of Asakura he was unable to repeat the generous gesture Toda Ippō had made to him some thirty years earlier. All he could do, as he made ready to continue his journey, was to encourage the young swordman to pursue his studies and express the wish that someday they might meet again.

Tenzen's immediate sense of loss was soon washed away by other, for his clan far more pressing, matters. The duel between the two warriors was fought on a peninsula stricken by conflict. Already the northern regions of the Bōsō Peninsula were immersed in civil war. Before long the southern half, too, would go under in the terrible tide of anarchy that had been set in motion a century before by the Ōnin

War. Soon all that Tenzen had known and grown up with would be swept away. It would uproot the young man and leave him stranded, as it had left Itō Ittōsai Kagehisa and so many other famous warriors of the Warring States period stranded. Like them, he would be thrown back on his own devices, with no more to rely upon than his sword, his techniques of the Mikami-ryū, and the few precious lessons he had learned that day in the gardens of the local hostel.

It was early in March 1588, as the little winter snow that fell on the peninsula was melting under the bright rays of a warm Pacific sun that the peace on the Mikogami estate was disturbed by a messenger from their Mangi castle that the Mikogami were to mobilize for war once more.

To the old Tosa the news came not as a big surprise. In spite of the truce between the Satomi and the Hōjō clans the peninsula had not been at peace, and as half a century before, it was again a feud within the Satomi clan that had fueled the unrest. On his deathbed Satomi Yoshihiro had ordained that the Satomi live in peace with the Hōjō, and that the estates be evenly divided between his brother, Yoshiyori, and his five year old son, Umeōmaru. His brother, who had long been the lord of Okamoto castle, near the port of Tomiura, was to become lord of the Satomi domains in the north, while his son was to inherit the domains in the south. When, however, Yoshihiro passed away, Yoshiyori seized the reins of control over the clan. For a while the young infant was raised at the Biwakubi Yakata,

The Yōrō River

the clan's large and luxurious mansion on the banks of the Yōrō River, which winds its way through the mountainous heart of the Bōsō peninsula. But when, in 1583, the infant reached boyhood, he was summoned to Okamoto castle, where under the watchful eyes of his jealous uncle, his head was forceably shaved and he was packed off to a local monastery, to spend the rest of his life in enforced exile.

There was no doubt in Tosa's mind that only the military power of the Toki had thus far kept Satomi Yoshiyori from intruding on their lands. It had been five years since their lord Toki Tameyori had passed away. He had been succeeded by his son Yoriharu, a youth with great strategic insight and equally determined to use his talent to maintain if not to expand his territories. He had not dared attack Ōtaki castle, which was now under control of the Satomi, but with the help of the Hōjō he had subdued a number of warlords whose domains bordered on his own. In this he had made considerable headway, spreading his sphere of influence toward the coast, to Ōhara and its stronghold Kobama castle. Thankfully, its master, Yarita Katsutada, had subjected to Yoriharu's will and proven a reliable vassal. The capture of Kobama castle was a great asset to the Toki. Though not as big as the ports of Kamogawa and Katsura, Ōhara was an important port along the peninsula's east coast. As of late it had been a busy port, too. Encouraged by the truce between the Satomi and the Hōjō, more and more merchant vessels had rounded the peninsula carrying goods from afar afield as Nagoya, Sakai, and Osaka.

A new mood of optimism had swept through the Kantō during the decade that had passed since Satomi Yoshiro's death. Takeda Shingen, Uesugi Kenshin, and Hōjō Ujiyasu, the great warlords of the Warring States period, had all passed away. Their successors differed little in their outlook and ambitions, yet none of them had the military genius of their fathers, and thus their military limitations forced them to achieve their aims through more peaceful means.

The promontory on which once stood Kobama castle

65

Partly out of self interest and partly to appease the spirit of his dead brother, Yoshiyori had made serious efforts to improve the ties between his clan and the Hōjō. He had taken as his wife the beautiful Sakuhime, the sister of Hōjō Ujimasa. The latter, too, was keen on a rapprochement, for like the Satomi, much of the wealth and power of the Hōjō depended on the vast merchant fleet that plowed the waves of Edo Bay. The shipping routes along which they sailed were part of a huge network that enveloped all the main islands of the Japanese realm, all the way from the island of Hirado, off Kyūshū's west coast, up to Aomori, the most northern port of call on the main island of Honshū. Together with the bays of Osaka and Ise, Edo Bay was one of the most intensely trafficked waters in the Japanese isles. There were dozens of ports along its shores alone, and many more along the major rivers of the Kantō. Then there were, of course, the ports around the Bōsō Peninsula, many of which were under the control of the Satomi.

Japanese merchantman from the 16th century

The battle for the Ishiyama Hongan

Throughout the Warring States period, in spite of the internecine wars that raged on land, the merchantmen had continued to frequent their familiar ports of call, even when they now fell under the control of enemy warlords. The latter's dependence on that very trade to conduct their wars meant that, apart from levying taxes, they generally allowed entry into their ports. A far greater worry for the merchants was the threat of piracy. In an age of anarchy there were many independent pirates. The most feared among them were the notorious *wakō*. These, however, largely made their living by preying on the merchantmen that carried goods between Japan and the mainland. The majority of pirate ships operating along Japanese shores were in some way or other under the control of the great seagoing clans. Clans like the Mōri, who through their vast fleet of warships controlled all of the traffic on the Inland Sea. Their naval power had made it possible for the followers of the Ikkō sect to hold out so long against Oda Nobunaga's forces at the

67

Tateyama castle, the headquarters of Satomi Yoshiyori

Ishiyama Hongan monastery, which was situated on islands in the delta of the Yodo River.

Closer to home it had been the Miura who had long dominated the seas around the Miura Peninsula and beyond. With the death of Miura Tokitaka in 1494, their naval supremacy had come to an abrupt end. It was true that their end had come at the hands of the Uesugi, the clan of his adopted son, but the clans who had benefited most from the demise of the Miura were the Satomi and the Hōjō. It had been through Tokitaka's natural son, Michitsuna, after all, that the Satomi had acquired part of the Miura fleet and the seafaring knowledge that went with it. The Hōjō, too, had benefited, for one of the many castles they had subdued in their northward expansion had been that of Arai, the former Miura stronghold, and with its capture they had acquired the other remnant of the Miura fleet. These naval assets had enabled both clans to launch overseas attacks on each other's territories. It had also strengthened their economic power, for even though they allowed the merchantmen to frequent their ports unharmed, both clans engaged in a fair deal of unbridled piracy to replenish their ever dwindling war chests. They also turned a blind eye to the activities of other pirate ships, many of whom were the property of vassal clans like the Masaki, who operated from Katsura and other ports along the Awa coast. Here, too, Yoshiyori had sought to improve economic stability. Not long after Yoshihiro's death he had moved his headquarters to the port of Tateyama, from where many of the pirate ships operated. In 1578, he built Tateyama castle, a large castle overlooking Tateyama Bay, from where he began to clamp down on the pirates. At the same time he encouraged trade with merchants from Ise and father afield by issuing warrants of safe passage to the ships that called at Tateyama and were destined for ports in Awa and Kazusa.

For a decade Yoshiyori had managed to sustain his policy of appeasement abroad and economic revival at home, but the one was thwarted by the death of his wife and the other stalled following his own death in 1587. Only a year had passed since then, but in that year it had become abundantly clear that his successor, the fiercely belligerent Yoshiyasu, did not share his father's moderate views. Shortly after Yoshiyori's death, word reached Mangi castle that Yoshiyasu had broken the fragile truce that existed between the Satomi and the Hōjō. It was a development that affected the whole of the Kantō and, as such, the rest of the country, yet it was small clans like the Mikogami, whose estates were wedged between those of the powerful clans, who had benefited most

69

The fiercely belligerent Satomi Yoshiyasu, who sought to emulate his grandfather, Yoshihiro

from their appeasement, and who now stood to lose the most by their alienation. To Tosa's dismay, the news that the messenger was carrying confirmed all the misgivings about his clan's immediate future that he had harbored since the demise of Yoshiyori and the rise of Yoshiyasu.

The messenger from Mangi castle related how, only weeks before, Satomi Yoshiyasu had launched a new campaign against the Hōjō, not northward into Kazusa, nor even across the Uraga Straits, toward the Miura Peninsula. Mobilizing his clan's remaining fleet of warships, he had instead crossed the Bay of Sagami, directly toward the Izu Peninsula and the Hōjō heartland. He had landed at Atami, a small port at the head of the peninsula. The port was controlled by Ajiro castle, whose lord, Kotōda Toshinao, was a vassal of the Hōjō. The castle itself was only a minor stronghold, but it played a pivotal role in the military campaigns of the Hōjō, as it acted as a relay station between Odawara and their other castles on the other side of the peninsula. As yet the castle had not fallen, but Toshinao was unable to rely on the help of the Hōjō, as they were tied down elsewhere. Instead he had called in the help of Toki Yoriharu, who, due to his connections with the Hōjō, was obliged to assist in the defence of Ajiro castle.

The contingent was to sail under the command of Yarita Katsutada, the lord of Kobama castle, chiefly because of his naval expertise, but also to test his loyalty toward his new overlords. Already Katsutada had assembled at Ōhara, a small fleet of merchantmen with which to ferry his warriors around the peninsula and relieve the besieged forces at Atami. They included the strongest and most able of the Toki warriors, among them those of the house of Mikogami.

Mikogami Tosa had engaged in countless battles on behalf of his lord. He had fought his first battle way back in 1534, on the plain of Inukake. Now, however, he was an old man, and though he could still command a force in the field on horseback, he was too weak and frail to embark on such a long and arduous journey. And thus it fell to Tenzen to follow in his father's footsteps and uphold the honor of the Mikogami clan. Seeing his son take on these responsibilities filled the old Tosa with great pride. Yet it was also with great reluctance that the Mikogami patriarch sent his son on his way. Even as he visited the local Shintō shrine to make votive offers and pray for his son's safe return, something deep down in his heart told him that he had probably set his eyes on his son for the last time.

For the twenty-four-year-old Tenzen this was the chance of a lifetime. Not yet had he actively participated in any battle, let alone taken part in any military campaign that was being conducted over sea. The enterprise had also a senti-

Sagami Bay

72

The unforgiving cliffs of the Atami shore

mental side to it, for Tenzen had been raised on the old tales, transmitted down the generations by word of mouth, of how, more than a century ago, his distant ancestor, Tōchi Ōtoshi, too, had crossed the sea, without knowing what awaited him on the other side of the water.

The passage was a safe one. The decade of peace between the Satomi and the Hōjō and Yoshiyori's clampdown had forced the pirates who had operated in the area to either look elsewhere or to abandon their evil ways and turn their attention to trade. As a result, Yoshiyasu had been unable to mobilize the kind of fleet that had sailed under the command of his grandfather Yoshihiro. He had also been too ambitious in his goal. Instead of attacking the Hōjō positions on the Miura Peninsula, where their lines of supply were long and thin, he had chosen to fight far away from home, where he himself was unable to replenish his troops. Though badly defended, Ajiro castle, which overlooked the Bay of Ajiro, lay at the center of the Hōjō heartland, less

73

Ajiro Bay

than ten miles from their headquarters of Odawara. Even if he were to capture the castle, the Hōjō would never allow him to hang on to his foothold. It was for that reason that, upon their arrival, Tenzen and his fellow men found that they had been preceded by a small contingent of warriors from Odawara. With their help Kotōda Toshinao had been able to repel the Satomi ships, which had retreated to a port further up the coast toward Itō.

Over the following months, as they prepared for the return of the Satomi ships, the two bands of warriors, thrown together by fate, gradually warmed to each other. Their dialects and customs differed remarkably, but as the weeks wore on and they grew accustomed to each other's peculiarities, the hurdles began to melt away. There were even the occasional nocturnal amusements, but much of the daytime was spent in the usual chores that came with the defense of a castle, the reinforcements of its defenses, the replenishment of provisions, the patrolling of the surrounding area, and the gathering of intelligence. During the hours that remained the warriors either rested or engaged in practice. All of the Hōjō men were able and well-trained warriors, at home with the *yari* as well as the longsword, but one among them stood out in particular. He was a sophisticated-looking man, at least twice Tenzen's age. For some reason the old man intrigued Tenzen from the moment he set eyes on him.

It appeared that the old warrior had been Kotōda Toshinao's fencing instructor for many years and had now come to his pupil's aid in the defense of Ajiro castle. Many tales were told about him. One recounted how, on his travels around the Miura Peninsula during the seventies, he had visited Misaki. The port of Misaki lay at the head of the Bay of Koajiro, not far from the Hōjō stronghold of Arai castle. It was an important port of call for Japanese merchant ships, as well as the occasional vessel from the Chinese mainland. According to the tale one such ship had been in port during the swordman's visit. It had carried a delegation of officials from the court of the Tang emperor, who were on their way to Odawara and guarded by a large number of Chinese imperial guards. The guards, so the story went, had been so boastful of their own and dismissive of the Japanese art of swordsmanship that the lone swordsman had challenged them to a duel: they with their broad and curved Chinese swords, he with his single Japanese *bokken* of hardwood. Drunk on *sake* and their own conceit, the guards had taken up the challenge, but when they had slept off their stupor and engaged the warrior in combat each and every one of them had been disarmed with a single stroke of the *bokken*. The tale had sent a shiver of recognition up Tenzen's spine as he felt his wrist and recounted his own humiliating defeat at a mere piece of wood. He was even more intrigued when he learned that the name by which this enigmatic warrior went was Toda Ittōsai. That name and the warrior's style of fencing immediately told Tenzen that somehow there must be a link between the old man and the warrior who had defeated him in the garden of the hostel.

It was not long before Tenzen found an occasion to speak to the old swordsman, and discovered that his real name was Kanemaki Jisai, the one-time tutor of Itō Ittōsai. Tenzen related how, five years before, Ittōsai had visited his village and how he had disarmed him in a single stroke. He expressed his deep admiration for the Toda and Ittō schools of fencing and beseeched the old man to reveal to him the secrets that his friend had not had the time to impart.

Until the end of 1588 Tenzen pursued his study of swordsmanship under Kanemaki Jisai's guidance, practicing the techniques of the Ittō, Toda, and Nen-ryū, and listening in rapture as his teacher recounted how these three schools of fencing formed a long line of progress in a tradition of swordsmanship that went all the way back to the middle of the fourteenth century, when, during the nationwide struggle between the two imperial courts, a young warrior like him had developed his own style of fencing to avenge the death of his father. This, for Tenzen so formative a period, came to an abrupt end early in January 1589, when Jisai told him that he was leaving Ajiro castle. The old swordsman had been invited to Odawara castle by none other than Hōjō Ujimasa himself. It seemed that down south in the capital forces were gathering against the Hōjō, and they needed all the help they could get.

At their parting, as the old mercenary made ready to set off along the coast toward Odawa, he impressed on Tenzen the need to widen his intellectual horizons and pursue his martial studies. To this purpose he handed him a letter of recommendation to Obata Masamori, the garrison commander of Kaizu castle, the stronghold of Kōsaka Masanobu, one of Takeda Shingen's chief commanders in the province of Shinano. Masamori, he assured him, was a formidable swordsman in his own right, but even more knowledgable in the field of *heihō*, the art of warfare, in which his father had founded a school named the Kōshū-ryū, whose teachings had played a major role in Shingen's incredible successes on the field of battle. Jisai had visited Kaizu

Kaizu castle, breeding ground of the Kōshū-ryū

castle with Toda Shigemasa and Itō Ittōsai after they had fled across the Aburazaka pass. At that time Masamori had still been in his forties, and as far Jisai knew he was still living at Kaizu castle.

For Tenzen, too, the time had come to return home. Word had reached the castle that the new Satomi leader had given up on his adventure. His ships had left the Izu coast and headed out to sea, almost surely back to Awa and the port of Tateyama. And thus late in January, Tenzen and his fellow warriors readied their ships, cast off from Ajiro castle, and set sail for home.

The naval expedition had not gone unnoticed at home, especially in Katsura. There the new lord of Katsura castle, Masaki Yoritada, had observed a large fleet creeping southward along the horizon. His informants had already told him that the Toki had been gathering forces farther north along the coast, at Ohara, and he had quickly put two and two together: the Toki were either under way to launch a seaborne raid on the Satomi heartland in Awa, or they had come to the aid of the Hōjō on the other side of Edo Bay—both scenarios were fine with him.

For a long time the Masaki had had their eyes on the Toki domains, yet their great chance of 1575, when Satomi Yoshihiro had ordered his father to seize Mangi castle, had been an abject failure. It had been a double failure, for not only had they lost many of their men, but it had also seriously undermined their relation with the Satomi, who were

View from Katsura castle

already suspicious of the Masaki's loyalty. Over the previous decades the Masaki domains had repeatedly come under the influence of the Hōjō. Shortly after the second battle at Konodai, when the Hōjō had penetrated deep into the peninsula, Masaki Tokishige, then still lord of their family stronghold of Ōtaki castle, had been forced to submit to their will. Down south at Katsura Masaki Tokitada had been safe, but to ensure his brother's safety he had sent his son to Odawara to serve as hostage. For several years Yoritada had remained at Odawara, until, in the wake of the battle of Mifune, he was exchanged for a Hōjō hostage and able to succeed his father as lord of Katsura castle.

Such coming and going of hostages between allied clans was a common enough practice in the uncertain times in which they lived, but the Satomi had put the stamp of betrayal on what had been an act of desperation. The Masaki had fought hard to rid themselves of the stigma, but their failure to reduce Mangi castle had eclipsed their successes at

79

Mifune. Tokishige's adopted successor, Noritoki, had even given up trying and turned against his former lord. Hearing of the death of the Satomi chieftain, he had taken up the cause of the rightful Satomi heir and attacked a number of Yoshiyori's strongholds in the peninsula's central region, including Kanayama castle. Not much later his troops appeared on the peninsula's east coast, where they attacked Katsurayama, Okitsu, and Yoshiuji, all strongholds that were under the control of his stepbrother Yoritada. The speed with which all this was done struck terror into the peninsula's dwellers, but also a degree of admiration, for soon Noritoki became the subject of legends in which he was attributed superhuman powers.

For a long time Yoritada had been hard pressed, holding out at his one remaining stronghold of Katsura, while send-

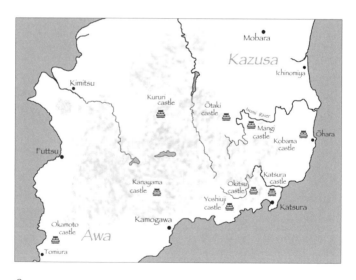

Masaki Noritoki, the subject of legends

ing messengers to Okamoto castle for Yoshiyori's help. His predicament was resolved in 1581, when Yoshiyori rode out in force and began to lay siege to the castles that Yoritada had made his own. At length Noritoki had been forced to withdraw to the family stronghold of Ōtaki castle. His powers, in the end, were those of a mortal; betrayed by one of his own men, he was slain in an ambush that same year.

With Noritoki's death the castles of Kanayama and Ōtaki had again fallen into the hands of the Satomi, and it was with their help that Yoritada was able to reestablish his control over his former strongholds south of Katsura. As of late he had even turned his attention northward, toward Ōhara and the Toki domains.

Now, as he watched the fleet of ships creep southward along the horizon from the upper donjon of Katsura castle, he saw how the Toki domains might finally be his. With many of their ablest fighting men away, the Toki defenses would be seriously compromised, and he calculated that

81

especially at Ōhara it would take only a minor force to evict them from Kobama castle. A week before, when his informants had first spotted the Toki troop movements between Ōtaki and Ōhara, he had immediately dispatched a messenger across the peninsula to notify the Satomi of his intentions, and only a few days later he received Yoshiyasu's written approval. By then he had already assembled a force of some one hundred fifty mounted warriors, and several more *ashigaru*. Shortly after they had watched the mastheads of Yarita Katsutada's ships disappear below the southern horizon, Yoritada and his men rode out from Katsura castle. When they reached the town's outskirts they broke into a gallop, hurrying northward along the coast, toward the port of Ōhara and Kobama castle.

It was late in February 1589 when Yarita Katsutada's fleet of ships returned to Ōhara. Exactly a year had passed since they had set sail—a year in which they had experienced various hardships. Nothing, however, prepared him and his men for the spectacle that awaited them on their arrival. From afar they could see the Masaki banner flying from the upper moat of Kobama castle and when the shallow ships drew near to the coast the Portuguese cannon that had been Katsutada's proud possessions were now turned against them. Through the haze above the Pacific surf they could make out a large force awaiting them on the beach, their colored suits of armor set off against the white sand, and the polished metal of their lances glimmering in the cold

February light. There were at least several hundred men and so Katsutada ordered his fleet to sail on, farther north along the coast, until they had reached the mouth of the Isumi River. From there they sailed upriver, toward Isumi, where they hoped to hear news of Mangi castle.

That evening, exhausted by the long journey and deeply troubled by the scene they had encountered at Ōhara, Katsutada and his men reached the village of Isumi. When they had finally tied up their boats and landed their gear, they were met by the village elder, and it was with a painful mixture of relief and apprehension that they listened as the old man described in exhaustive detail the dramatic events of Masaki Yoritada's cowardly attack in the wake of their departure. The skeleton force that had guarded Kobama castle had been no match for Yoritada and his band of warriors.

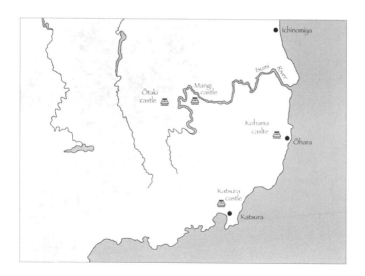

The head guard, still a young man, had sought to make up for his lack of experience through reckless bravery. Instead of waiting for reinforcements from Mangi castle, he had ordered the few troops he had to take the field and face Yoritada's men head on. It was a terrible mistake and one for which he paid a high price, for that day he and most of his men were driven into the sea and slaughtered to a man.

Five months after Masaki Yoritada had subdued Kobama castle, he used the old family stronghold of Ōtaki castle to launch an attack into Toki territory. It was a far more thoroughly prepared campaign that the ad hoc assault by which he had captured Kobama castle. During the five months preparation he had mobilized all the troops his vassals could muster, and had pressed many of Yarita's clansmen into service. In doing so he raised close to three thousand troops. These he moved to Ōtaki castle, from where he crossed the Isumi River in an attempt to finally capture Mangi castle. Given its situation along the Isumi River the Mikogami estate was immediately on their way and Tenzen's clan bore the full brunt of the attack.

It appeared that on the eve of the attack his father had been restless, plagued by premonitions. He had posted a number of his men along the river and sent the womenfolk and children to Mangi castle. He himself and the rest of the Mikogami warriors had withdrawn into the forest and taken up vigil. His vigilance paid off. Early next morning, well before the sun had risen, his scouts reported that Masaki Yoritada had led a vast army across the Isumi River. They estimated that there were some three thousand warriors,

The Isumi River where it skirts the Mangi estate

most of whom were on foot. Holding their swords above their heads, they had waded through the cool river water, and stealthily climbed the opposite banks. There they had assembled and set off in the direction of Mangi castle. A small contingent had separated from the main body and followed a Masaki warrior on horseback. It had been difficult to make out in the dark, but the scout who had seen him believed that it was Tokishige, the son of Masaki Noritoki, and the new master of Ōtaki castle. Whoever it was he had led his men directly toward the Mikogami mansion. Hearing this, Tosa had ordered the majority of his clansmen to make straight for Mangi castle, warn their lord of the pending attack, and help in the castle's defense. Only twenty of his best men he had kept with him. Then he had sped off in the direction of the Mikogami mansion. It was the last time Tosa was ever seen alive, but thanks to Tosa's prescience Masaki Yoritada's surprise attack failed. Familiar with the terrain, the Mikogami warriors reached Mangi castle well before the enemy and with their help the Toki had repelled the initial attack.

Undaunted by his initial setback, Yoritada had thrown up a cordon around Mangi castle hoping to starve his enemy to death. He had been joined by the Yamakawa, another clan alieged to the Satomi. They controlled Maru castle, in Tenzen's ancestral hometown of Maruyama. The Mikogami possessions in Maruyama had long since been confiscated by the Yamakawa, and now Tenzen had to learn how, during the year that he had been away, all that he, his father, and his ancestors had built up with much toil in Isumi had also been confiscated by his clan's enemies.

As the siege dragged on Yoritada had put his men to work on the construction of a large *mukaijō*, a facing stronghold to which his forces could withdraw, recuperate, and launch a fresh attack. It was built on the slopes of what the locals referred to as Mount Hachiban. No more than a hill, it was situated halfway between the castle and the Isumi River, right at the center of the Mikogami estate. The materials from which it was built had been taken from buildings in the surrounding area, including the mansion and outbuildings of the Mikogami clan, which had all been razed to the ground. All the effort had done, however, was to stave off Yoritada's defeat. Time and time again the Toki repelled the attacks, causing huge casualties among Yoritada's men. They also repeatedly managed to breach the cordon, establishing a fragile supply route over the river that held sufficiently long for them to replenish the castle's supplies with fresh victuals. Yoritada's hopes of a final breakthrough dissolved when his ally decided he had seen enough killing and ordered his troops home. Eventually winter had set in, forcing Yoritada, too, to concede defeat and withdraw his weary and demoralized troops behind the Isumi River.

These tidings were a grave blow to the young Tenzen. He now knew that his father, brothers, and most of his closest family members had died in battle. From what he learned from the village elder and the few surviving Mikogami clansmen, Tenzen was able to reconstruct what had happened to his father during his last moment on earth. Enemy warriors who had been captured during the siege had spoken of fierce fighting around the Mikogami mansion on the night of the surprise attack. It seemed that Masaki Tokishige and his men had run into stiff opposition while on their way to Mangi castle. They had been forced to retreat to Mount Iwashō, where they had come to blows once more. In the melee, Tokishige himself had clashed several times with another mounted warrior. The man had clearly been

Today Mount Hachiban is marked by the eponymous shrine

advanced in years, yet only with the help of several other Masaki warriors had Tokishige finally gotten the better of him. The fighting had dragged on until the morning light and the attacking warriors, some twenty men in all, had been slain to a man. Many of Tokishige's own men, too, had died, the majority of them archers. Their brief had been to make a circular movement and fire incendiary arrows into the exposed woodwork at the back of the castle, where it was least guarded. In the dense undergrowth they had been unable to use their bows to full advantage, and less able with the sword, many of them had perished.

The account of his father's heroic death filled the young warrior with great pride, yet it also greatly afflicted his conscience. He fully realized that his presence would have made little difference, but had he only been there, at least he would have fought and died alongside his father—an honorable end for any warrior. Now he had to come to terms with the death of his loved ones, and to his warrior's mind there was only one way to expiate his sense of guilt and that was through the device of *musha shugyō*. And thus, in the early spring of 1590, the young warrior took his leave from Toki Yoriharu and set off on his martial pilgrimage. His first destination was the small but famous town of Sawara, and the famous Katori shrine, the birthplace of the illustrious Iizasa Chōisai Ienao, the founder of the Shintō school of fencing. From there he would cross the Sea of Katori, to visit the village of Kashima, where he intended to worship and practice at the Kashima shrine, that other place of worship so closely connected to the Shintō-ryū and its great propagator

Tsukahara Bokuden. Then he would go up to Edo, from where he would travel up the Nakasendō, the old inland route to Kyoto. His final destination was Kaizu castle, the home of Obata Masamori, the great scholar of the art of warfare. He still had Kanemaki Jizai's letter of introduction and intended to make good use of it. As he set out from the village of Isumi toward the north, and the upper moat of Mangi castle slowly receded into the distance, Tenzen was both elated and apprehensive, aware that his past was gone forever and not sure what the future had in store for him.

Japan at the time Tenzen set out on his journey was undergoing great changes. The drive toward centralized control that had been set in motion by Oda Nobunaga, when he had seized the capital in the autumn of 1568, had gone on relentlessly. Having defeated the Asai and the Asakura, he had gone on to destroy the belligerent Tendai and Ikkō, the Buddhist sects that had given him such trouble. Many of the warlords who had opposed his rise had been subdued, A number, such as the western warlord Mōri Terumoto, still resisted. Others, such as Takeda Shingen, had solved part of his problems by passing away. Nor did Nobunaga himself live to see his dream "to rule the whole country by force" fully materialize. In 1582 he was assassinated by one of his henchmen, Akechi Mitsuhide, who ambushed him during his stay at the Honnō temple in Kyoto. By that time only the middle regions of the Japanese archipelago had been brought under central control. Outlying regions such as the islands of Kyushu and Shikoku, as well as the western and northern extremities of Honshu were still under the control of local warlords.

When Nobunaga was killed, his general Toyotomi Hideyoshi had been pinned down in Bitchū, trying hard but failing to reduce Takamatsu castle, a center of western opposition. When he learned of Nobunaga's death, he immediately sued for peace, marched on the capital, and killed the treacherous Mitsuhide. Now it was left to him to continue Nobunaga's work, and he did so in brilliant fashion. Though, like Nobunage, a native of Owari province, he moved his headquarters to the centrally situated city of Osaka from where he could control the capital's approaches from the west. Shortly after his arrival he began on the construction of a huge castle on the grounds of the former Ishiyama Hongan monastery. At the same time he began to make plans for a series of vast military campaigns to subdue Japan's remote regions. The first, launched in 1585, was

Osaka castle, the new headquarters of Toyotomi Hideyoshi

Toyotomi Hideyoshi, the general who inherited Nobunaga's immense task

directed toward the provinces of Kii and Izumi, as well as the island of Shikoku. Shikoku proved an easy task, but his next goal, the remote island of Kyushu, less so. It took an army of some two hundred thousand troops, many of them armed with flintlock firearms to bring the island's rebellious warlords to heel. They finally surrendered in the summer of 1587. Hideyoshi was so successful in his campaigning that by the end of the nineties he had subdued as many as thirty provinces. Only the eastern regions of Japan had not yet been brought within the fold of centralized control.

The greatest threat to Hideyoshi's authority now came from the east, in particular from the Kantō plain, where the Hōjō were still in control. To curb their influence he had already forged alliances with rival clans in the region, the Satake of Hitachi, the Utsunomiya of Shimotsuke, and the Satomi of Awa. He was not keen on another great confrontation as the Hōjō were a formidable enemy and neither Uesugi Kenshin, nor Takeda Shingen had managed to subdue

*Odawara castle, headquarters
of the proud Hōjō*

their stronghold of Odawara. He even made several peaceful overtures to Hōjō Ujimasa, but all he received in reply were words of defiance. If, however, he was to realize his goal of a unified Japan he had to bring the Hōjō to heel. There was also a powerful economic incentive to do so. The Kantō was one of Japan's most fertile regions, and the territories of the Hōjō alone had an annual rice yields of more than three million *koku*. And thus he began to make plans for an equally vast campaign to bring the country's eastern regions under his control. Those plans reached their fruition in the winter of 1589, when he convened a council at the newly completed Osaka castle, and declared that the time had come for Ujimasa's head "to be removed."

Hideyoshi's preparations for his Kantō campaign were on an even grander scale than his Kyushu campaign. Orders for mobilization were sent to all the provinces under his control. Together they mustered more than two hundred thousand troops. He intended to move these forces against the Hōjō power base of Odawara castle and, anticipating a long, drawn out siege, he made elaborate preparations to sustain it for as long as it might take. Huge amounts of rice for his soldiers, as well as millet and fodder for their horses, were stored at Shimizu in Suruga. These were not to be carried over land across the dangerous Hakone Pass, but loaded onto a vast fleet provided by the Mōri, which would carry them around the Izu peninsula when required. In any event, his preparations proved superfluous. After only a few months Ujimasa surrendered, and he and his brother Ujiteru were forced to commit suicide.

For more than a century the Hōjō had dominated the political landscape in the Kantō. They had started out as a small clan of warriors in the service of the Ashikaga, with no more to their name than a few hectares of land on the Isu Peninsula. At the height of their power they had ruled supreme over the provinces of Musashi, Izu, Sagami, Kōzuke, Shimotsuke, Shimōsa, and Kazusa. All those possessions, all that wealth and prestige, had been lost in just a few months. The campaign had begun early in April 1590, only a few weeks after Tenzen departed from Isumi. It had ended on August 4, shortly before thirty-five-year-old warrior arrived in Edo in the blazing heat of summer.

Edo in 1590 was a bustling city and much of that energy emanated from its center of power, Edo castle. When Tenzen first set sight on its imposing splendor Edo castle was already more than a hundred years old. It had been built

93

Edo castle, Tokugawa Ieyasu's new headquarters

in 1457 by Ōta Dōkan, the great strategist and architect who had been employed by the Bakufu to build a line of defense against the belligerent *kantō kubō* Ashikaga Shigeuji. Dōkan had been in the service of the powerful Uesugi. He had been one of their most successful generals, but thirty years later he became embroiled in one of their internal feuds and was assassinated by a rival clan member. Perhaps it had been that act of treachery that caused his grandson, Ōta Suketaka, to turn against the Uesugi and recapture the castle for the Hōjō in 1524. Since then the town and its castle had been under their control, but now, to Tenzen's utter astonishment, it was not a Hōjō vassal, but Tokugawa Ieyasu who was lord of Edo castle.

The little that Tenzen had heard about Ieyasu was completely at odds with this new and bewildering state of affairs. As far as Tenzen knew, Ieyasu hailed from the province of Mikawa. He was the son of Matsudaira Hirotada, a small local chieftain, whose lands were hemmed in between those

94

of the powerful Oda of Owari and Imagawa of Suruga. Ieyasu was born and raised at the family headquarters of Okazaki castle, but in 1547, when they had suffered a defeat at the hands of the Oda, his father had sought protection with the Imagawa and sent the five-year-old Ieyasu to live among the Imagawa household as a hostage. On his way there he had been captured by an Oda vassal and instead sent to Owari. For two years the young Ieyasu had been held captive by the Oda, years during which his father died, and the fortunes of the Matsudaira rapidly dwindled. A truce between the two neighboring clans had led to his release, but no sooner was he set free than he was captured by Imagawa Yoshimoto. During his stay in Suruga he came of age and married one of Yoshimoto's daughter, but even then he was not allowed to return to Okazaki castle, and had remained at the mercy of the Imagawa until 1560. In that year Oda Nobunaga had killed Yoshimoto in the battle of Okehazama, and the thirteen-year-old Ieyasu was finally able

Okazaki castle, birthplace of Tokugawa Ieyasu

95

to succeed his father as lord of Okazaki castle. Grateful for his release, Ieyasu proved a reliable ally to Nobunaga and it had been that alliance that enabled him to become master of Mikawa within seven years of his release. By then he was already widely famed throughout Japan by his new family name of Tokugawa, the "river of virtue."

Now, as he was slurping his buckwheat noodles in a busy *sobaya* on one of Edo's great thoroughfares, Tenzen quickly learned that Ieyasu had come a long way since he had joined forces with Oda Nobunaga and crushed the Asai and Asakura at Ane River in 1570, though it had been a road with many pitfalls. Two years later, when he and Nobunaga had fought with Takeda Shingen on the plains of Mikata, they had suffered a crushing defeat, and it had been with only a handful of men that he had managed to reach the safety of his nearby headquarters of Hikuma castle in Hamamatsu. Shingen, of course, immediately attacked the castle, but when those within had built a huge fire on the inner court

Edo as it was in Tenzen's days

and sounded the huge *taiko* drums from the upper donjon, he had become apprehensive and withdrawn.

It had been a narrow escape, but fortune was with Ieyasu that day, as it would be on so many subsequent occasions, such as, for instance a decade later, when he was visiting Sakai, making merry with an old-time friend. Informed of Nobunaga's assassination, he had secretly left the port and made his way back to his headquarters in Hamamatsu. Aware of Hideyoshi's strength, he had not challenged his authority, but instead turned his attention to strengthening his position in the region. Those efforts led him to forge dangerous alliances, such as with Nobuna's second son, Nobukatsu, who was far from pleased with Hideyoshi's rapid rise. In 1584, the alliance had even led to direct confrontations between Ieyasu's and Hideyoshi's forces, first at Komakiyama, and then at Nagakute. Fortunately, neither confrontation led to a serious clash, as both men were wise enough not to let the dark broodings of others cloud their own horizons. Yet it had taught them each other's strength and the necessity of cooperation. Following these standoffs, the two men made peace and Ieyasu proved a trusted ally, especially in those instances where it helped to increase his own influence along the eastern seaboard. For that purpose he had also reached out toward the Hōjō, forging an alliance with Ujimasa in the following year. Over subsequent years, when Hideyoshi began to turn his attention eastward, Ieyasu worked hard to salvage his position by mediating between the two parties, but all his soothing words landed on death ears.

It had been with some reluctance, then, that, in the spring of 1590 Ieyasu moved his troops north along the Tōkaidō after he had been ordered by Hideyoshi to join in the siege of Odawara castle. Yet his choice had paid off. With the fall of Odawara and the demise of the Hōjō their territories had become part of the spoils of war, to be carved up and distributed among the victor's allies. It was probably with a view to appease Ieyasu that Hideyoshi had refrained from doing so and granted him all of the Hōjō territories. It was also a shrewd move, strengthening his own position, for in return Ieyasu had to give up his control over Suruga, Tōtōmi, his beloved Mikawa, as well as Kai and Shinano, the provinces he had wrested from the Takeda. Patient and far-sighted, Ieyasu had again complied with Hideyoshi's wishes. He made Edo castle his new headquarters, and quartered his closest vassals in the surrounding districts.

The great amount of information that Tenzen had learned in such a little space of time had thoroughly upset his plans. The main purpose of his journey was to seek out Obata Masamori at Kaizu castle. Takeda Shingen was dead and from what Tenzen had learned the former Takeda strongholds, including Kaizu castle, were now either under the control of Hideyoshi, Ieyasu, or one of their vassals. Could it be that Obata Masamori was still at Kaizu castle and serving its new master? It was highly unlikely, yet it was the only place where he could expect to find a clue concerning the scholar's whereabouts. And thus Tenzen set off from

Nihonbashi, center of Japan's main traffic arteries

Nihonbashi, the place where Japan's main traffic arteries met, taking the Kawagoe Kaidō, the old road that passed the historic castle town of Kawagoe and joined the Nakasendō at the old post town of Kumagaya.

It was not long after he had left Edo, while Tenzen was passing through Hizaori, a hamlet of no more than a few dozen peasant dwellings, that he came upon a scene of great confusion. A *rōnin* had killed a number of villagers in a dispute and was hiding out in a local farmhouse. Already one of Ieyasu's officials had arrived on the scene, but no one dared to approach the farmhouse, fearful as they were of the murderous villain. Unruffled by the commotion, and even less impressed with the villain's behavior, Tenzen approached the official, a young man, not even in his twenties, offering to resolve the matter, and it was not without relief that the young man accepted.

The *Honchō bugei shōden*, written more than a century after the events of that day by the martial historian Hinatsu

99

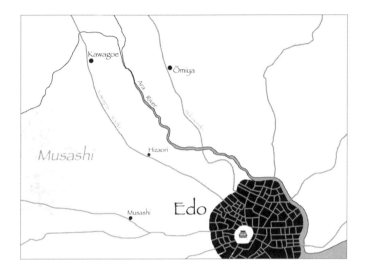

Shigetaka, describes the event in remarkable detail. According to Shigetaka, Tenzen moved toward the dwelling and cried out "I am Mikogami Tenzen and I have come from Edo by order of the shogun, do you wish to fight me, or should I come in?" Shigetaka goes on to claim that the villain, who up till then had been cowering inside, unwilling to face a group of peasants, replied that "for long I have been hearing about you, Tenzen, and being able to meet you is surely the best moment of my life. I shall come out and we shall duel." Having said this, "the swordsman came out and drew his longsword. Tenzen drew a sword only two *shaku* in length and promptly cut off the man's hands." Then, turning to the official, he asked, "Should I behead him or not?" When the latter nodded, "Tenzen cut off the criminal's head," and "the crowd was astonished."

It is impossible to ascertain the veracity of Shigetaka's account. What is certain is that, whatever took place at the small town of Hizaori on that summer's day in 1590, the incident formed the basis for a remarkable friendship, for the young official who had relied on Tenzen's help turned out to be none other than Obata Kagenori, a son of the very man Tenzen had set out to find.

When Tenzen handed Kagenori the letter of recommendation that Kanemaki Jisai had addressed to Kagenori's father the young man accepted it as if it was a message from the distant past. His father, he explained, had long since passed away. Kaizu castle had indeed been subdued by Nobunaga, but following his assassination at Honnō temple the stronghold had fallen into the hands of Uesugi Kagekatsu, an adoptive son of the great Kenshin. The shrewd Kagekatsu had heeded Hideyoshi's summons and joined in the siege of Odawara, a move that enabled him to hold on to his territories in Kai. Some members of Kagenori's clan had submitted to Kagekatsu's rule, but none of them had shown much interest or aptitude for Masamori's teachings. The responsibility of preserving his father's intellectual heritage now rested solely with him, and he would be delighted to share his insights with his newly won friend. For the moment, however, Tenzen needed a roof over his head, and here, too, the young official was able to help out, for he knew a good address in Hongō, at the center of town, and not far removed from Edo castle. The rent, he reassured the young warrior would be taken care of by his office, for good swordsmen like him were in high demand in these unruly times. He himself was an assistant to Amano Yasukage, who had just been appointed as Edo's *machi bugyō*, or metropolitan magistrate, responsible for running the city's day to day affairs and the maintaining of order. As the incident had proven, that office currently had its hand full in ridding the populace of surplus weapons.

Over the next few weeks, as he settled in his new surroundings and got acquainted with his fellow dwellers, Tenzen learned that the old Kanemaki Jisai had passed away. He had reached Odawara castle, but had fallen ill soon afterward. There was good news too. Jisai's two old friends, Toda Shigemasa and Itō Ittōsai, were still alive. Following their escape from Ichijōdani castle, Shigemasa had entered the service of Maeda Toshiie, who had helped Nobunaga to subjugate Echizen, and had become the lord of Fuchū castle, at the heart of the province. Ittōsai, it seemed, had meanwhile entered the service of Ōtani Yoshitsugu, who had helped Hideyoshi quell the unruly warlords on Kyushu. It

Toda Shigemasa, alias Yamazaki Saemon, Toda Seigen's star pupil

had only been a year since, that, in reward for his services, Hideyoshi had appointed Yoshitsugu as the lord of Tsuruga castle. Yoshitsugu, too, had taken part in the siege of Odawara. Currently, his forces were helping to police the redistribution of lands that Hideyoshi was conducting from Utsunomiya castle. Ittōsai was undoubtedly among them, but sooner or later he would pass through Edo on his way back to Tsuruga, and Tenzen would have the opportunity to meet the great swordsman once more.

Tenzen and the young official saw much of each other during the next few months, and it was in the course of these encounters that Kagenori told him the long and complicated story of his father's death. It was a tragic story, painful for Kagenori to recount, but it soon became clear to Tenzen that the events Kagenori described in such harrowing detail formed the driving force behind the young man's ambition.

Kagenori recounted how, following Takeda Shingen's death in 1573, his father's master, Kōsaka Masanobu, had remained in the service of the Takeda clan. His father, in turn, had continued to serve Masanobu as garrison commander at Kaizu castle. Having played an important role in Shingen's battles with Uesugi Kenshin at Kawanakajima and elsewhere, Masamori had also become the military advisor of Shingen's son, the clan's twentieth chieftain, Takeda Katsuyori. Though not possessed of his father's military genius, with Masamori's help, Katsuyori had continued to resist Nobunaga's drive toward central control. It had been

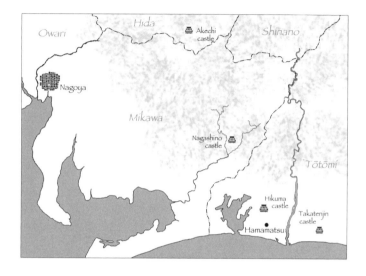

an uphill struggle for Katsuyori, as Nobunaga, who had just destroyed the Asai and the Asakura, seemed unstoppable. Masamori had warned his new lord of the threat, as well as that posed by Ieyasu, who, within months of Shingen's death, had captured Nagashino castle, some ten miles north of his own headquarters near Hamamatsu. The stronghold had fallen into the hands of the Takeda following Imagawa Yoshimoto's death and the clan's subsequent decline. Situated at the confluence of the Ono and Kansa rivers it had become the focal point of the Takeda and Tokugawa spheres of influence. What was needed, Masamori had advised his new lord, was a wide buffer of control to protect their territories from any further encroachments.

Katsuyori had carefully listened to his father's former advisor. Early in 1574, he marched into southern Hida at the head of some fifteen thousand men, and occupied Akechi castle, the headquarters of Akechi Mitsuhide, then still one of Nobunaga's allies. A few months later, having reduced a dozen other small strongholds, he had crossed the border with Tōtōmi and occupied Takatenjin castle, the stronghold of one of Ieyasu's vassals. For a while neither Nobunaga, nor Ieyasu moved, the former because he was tied down in the suppression of the Ikkō sectarians at Ishiyama and Nagashima, the latter because he did not have the means to expel Katsuyori. But when, in the spring of the following year, Katsuyori marched into Mikawa and laid siege of Nagashino castle, they had swung into action and pitched camp west of Nagashino with a combined force of close to forty thousand troops.

As Kagenori now knew, the battle of Nagashino had been a watershed in Japanese military history. Up until then, most of the battles had been fought in the traditional way: huge forces would be arrayed in several smaller units, usually those

Takeda Katsuyori

of a single clan and under the command of the clan's chieftain. The battle would usually commence with an exchange of arrows, fired from intermediate range. When one side launched an attack, it would do so in several waves, until, at length, the armies would clash, and a pitched battle developed in which soldiers would pick their man and engage in man-to-man combat. That was the way in which the great battles at Kawanakajima had been fought. It had formed the foundations of Masamori's Kōshū school of warfare, and it had been according to those tenets that, on May 21, the Takeda forces had opened the attack on their enemy.

Nobunaga, by then, had come to embrace a totally new way of warfare. His control over the capital and proximity to the port of Sakai had brought him into close contact with the Portuguese, who had arrived in Japan during the middle

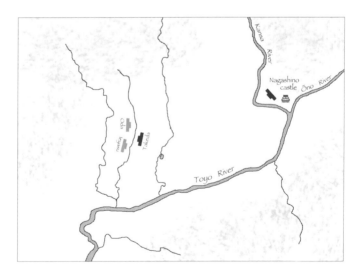

The Battle of Nagashino

of the sixteenth century. They had introduced a number of Western inventions, including the musket. Nobunaga had been one of the first warlords to fully recognize its potential on the field of battle. It was still a crude weapon, effective at no more than a hundred meters, muzzle-loaded, and fired by a spark from a tinder, but nevertheless superior to the ancient bow and arrow. To counter the musket's slow firing power, Nobunaga had divided his musketeers into three sections, which fired in rotation. This required great discipline, and he had spent a lot of time and effort to make the unruly *ashigaru* grow used to this regimented way of fighting. To counter his enemy's cavalry charges, he erected wooden palisades, too high for the horses to leap over then, and arranged in zigzag patterns to trap and disperse their ranks.

The introduction of all these innovations proved to be hugely effective. Brought up short against the high palisades Katsuyori's mounted warriors were shot down like lame ducks, defenseless as they were against the reach of the deadly muskets. Katsuyori managed to get away alive, but of the fifteen thousand men who had ridden into battle under his command two-thirds left their life at Nagashino. Many of his top commanders, too, had lost their lives, among them Naitō Masatoyo, the lord of Minowa castle.

Kagenori recounted to Tenzen how the crushing defeat at Nagashino had left his father a broken man. Masamori had seen the defeat as a personal failure. Almost overnight the splendid cavalry charges for which the Takeda had been so feared—and by which Nobunaga and Ieyasu had suffered such a humiliating defeat at Mikatagahara—had proven an impotent and anachronistic flurry from the past. He continued to serve Katsuyori as the master of Kaizu castle, but never again did he participate in any major battle. Instead, he looked on from afar, as if paralyzed, while his master desperately strove to restore what seemed irretrievably lost.

Those bleak and desperate years stood in dark relief with the glorious ones that had gone before; where Shingen had won victory upon victory, Katsuyori suffered setback after setback. These setbacks had culminated in the loss of Takatenjin castle to Ieyasu in 1581. At length Katsuyori had been forced to abandon even his headquarters of Tsutsujigasaki, right at the center of his home province of Kai. He had moved westward, toward Nirasaki, where he had begun the construction of Shinpu castle. Situated amid mountainous terrain, its strategic benefits were huge, but so were its costs, and some of his closest vassals, who were forced to bear the financial burden, turned against him and went over to Nobunaga's side.

The latter, by then, had finally succeeded in destroying the power bases of the Ikkō sectarians, and with the help of Ieyasu and his new allies, launched a large-scale campaign into Kai. The defection of Katsuyori's vassals had so impeded the building on Shinpu castle that it was too weak to withstand the kind of siege Nobunaga could muster. Torching his new castle, Katsuyori moved eastward, toward Iwadono castle, where he counted on the protection of his old vassal Oyamada Nobushige. By now he was not traveling but fleeing—into the arms of his enemies, it proved, for Nobushige, too, had betrayed his former lord and awaited him in force at the Sasago pass. Again Katsuyori changed direction, this time northward, in the hope of reaching the safety of Iwabitsu castle, in the province of Musashi. But now he found his retreat cut off by one of Nobunaga's generals,

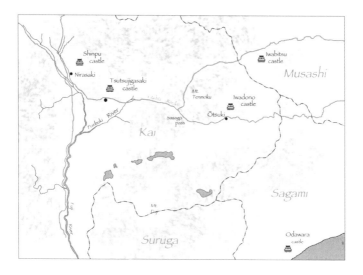

*Katsuyori's last moments
at the foot of Mount Tenmoku*

forcing him to retreat to the slopes of Mount Tenmoku. When he finally did find peace, it was not at the behest of one of his vassals, but by his own sword.

With the death of Katsuyori, his wife, and his son, the short but violent epoch of glory of the Takeda clan, an epoch that had begun so notoriously with Shingen's betrayal of his father, had come to a tragic close. For Masamori it had been all too much. Kagenori recalled how, upon the news of the fall of Tsutsujigasaki, his father had taken to his bed never to rise again. He died on March 30, 1582, five days before his lord committed ritual suicide on Mount Tenmoku. It had been a sad and ignominious end—an end from which Kagenori had been saved.

Kagenori at that time had only been ten years old, an infant even by the harsh and spartan standards of his time. With the fall of Kaizu castle, Ieyasu had taken pity on the boy and made him part of the retinue of his son, Hidetada. It had only been a few years since that he had come of age and formally entered Ieyasu's service, and only months since he had been promoted to his current position.

Ieyasu had proved a generous lord, in a way even a father to the young Kagenori. It was evident that, ever since his narrow escape at Mikatagahara, Ieyasu had been in deep awe of the Takeda and all who served them. Following Katsuyori's tragic death he had even vowed to build a mausoleum at the foot of Mount Tenmoku in honor of his fearsome foe (a vow he was to honor a few decades later). Kagenori had been allowed to pursue his father's studies. He had inherited much of his father's writings and was keen to advance his Kōshū school of warfare. On his departure from Kaizu castle he had also managed to rescue the writings of the lord of Kaizu castle, Kōsaka Masanobu, whose natural death in 1578 had saved him from the ignominy of the years that followed. Masanobu had served both Shingen and Katsuyori and had recorded his experiences and the clan's tactics and methods of warfare in a work he had given the

Tokugawa Ieyasu

title *Kōyō gunkan*. Though intimately familiar with his subject, Masanobu had not been a gifted writer and much of his work needed recasting. It was also huge in volume, hundreds of letters, notes, and unfinished drafts. Kagenori explained how he intended to combine the writings of his father and his master into a comprehensive work that would also carry the name *Kōyō gunkan*. He had already completed a large part and was delighted with the swordman's interest.

It was early in 1591 that Tenzen was visited by an unexpected guest, Itō Ittōsai Kagehisa. Most of the northern provinces had been pacified, and Kagehisa's lord, Ōtani Yoshitsugu, had returned to Tsuruga castle to help prepare the fleet for Hideyoshi's next and most ambitious plan—the invasion of Korea.

Kagehisa himself, however, had other plans. He had taken leave to embark on yet another *musha shugyō*. During his visit to the magistrate's office, he had heard of Tenzen's valuable work in dealing with troublemakers. Then, to Tenzen's surprise, the fencing master vividly recalled the duel they had fought in the garden of the Isumi hostel almost a decade before, for he referred to the encounter with fondness and commented on Tenzen's apparent progress. He explained that he wanted to travel to the Sōma district in the province of Shimōsa, where he intended to visit the remains of Fujigatani castle, the birthplace of Nenami Jion, the founder of the Nen-ryū which formed the basis for his own style of fencing. He had been told that Tenzen had traveled though

Shimōsa on his visit to the Kashima and Katori shrines and was curious whether he would care to join him. They would be joined by another swordsman, a certain Zenki, a man of brute strength but no great genius.

There was something in Ittōsai's behavior that Tenzen could not fathom. Equally inscrutable was the master's attitude to Zenki. Somehow it seemed to Tenzen that Ittōsai was suspicious of Zenki and favored his newly acquired disciple, an impression that was reinforced when the master warned him of Zenki's skill and offered to teach him the *musōken*, a technique that had come to him when, during a visit to Kamakura, he had spent a week in deep meditation at the Tsurugaoka Hachiman, the great shrine built by Minamoto Yoritomo to celebrate the defeat of the Taira. The *musōken*, he told his pupil, was a technique that transcended all others in that it relied, not on fixed movements, but on the most visceral instincts of its practitioner. It consisted of no more than a set of meditative techniques by

*The Tsurugaoka
Hachiman shrine*

113

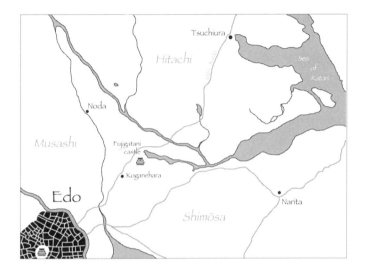

which one could release the powers of one's sixth sense and bring into perfect balance the spiritual and the physical realm. The ultimate goal of the exercise was to anticipate an opponent's action and react spontaneously, without the intervention of distracting and constraining thoughts. As such it formed the essence of the Japanese art of duelling, of which the outcome was decided by a warrior's fighting instincts rather than his intellectual superiority.

Though grateful, Tenzen was mystified as to why the master should impart these insights to him. Following the duel in the garden of the hostel at Isumi, Ittōsai had not deigned to cast even a glance at him. And why should he have? Had he not defeated the young upstart with a mere piece of old wood, beaten him with the proverbial stick? Yet there was something in the old man's behavior that now inspired

Tenzen with confidence. Could it be that in the ten years that had passed since that ignominious episode the master had changed his mind about him?

All these questions were finally answered when, traveling along the Mito Kaidō the three men arrived in a hamlet called Koganehara. They were now in the immediate vicinity of Fujigatani castle, and it seemed that the time had come for the old master to reveal to his disciples the true purpose of their pilgrimage. Again we have to rely on Hinatsu Shigetaka's *Honchō bugei shōden* for an account of that day's events. Shigetaka describes how, not long after their arrival in Koganehara:

> Ittōsai summoned Tenzen and Zenki, and told them, "I have been involved with swordsmanship since I was a child. While I travelled throughout the provinces few indeed were those who were my match. By this point in my life, I have now done all I wanted to and am satisfied. I shall now pass on my sword, the *Kamewari*. But one sword cannot be passed on to two people. I ask that you duel on this field to determine who is the better swordsman. I shall pass on my sword to whoever wins.

Sadly we know no more of the duel between the two protagonists of the Ittō school of fencing, except that it was Mikogami Tenzen who remained standing after this gruelling test on the plains of Kogane. For the aging Ittōsai, as well as for Tenzen, a warrior in the prime of his life, it was a moment fraught with great symbolic significance. More than two centuries ago the district of Sōma had been the birthplace of the

Nen-ryū, the school of fencing that had spawned the Toda-
ryū, the precursor to Ittōsai's Ittō-ryū. It had been along this
road that, in 1356, the young Sōma Yoshimoto had been
forced to flee into exile following the treacherous assassination of his father at the hands of Sōma Chikatane's henchmen. It had been along this road that the grown man had
returned fifteen years later, urged on by his desire to avenge
the death of his father. The soil on which they stood had
been stained by the blood of Nenami Jion's father, the leader
of the Shimōsa line of the Sōma clan, a stain that had been
washed away by the blood of Chikatane, the leader of the
Mutsu line of the Sōma clan.

During the next year Ittōsai and Tenzen spent a life on the
road in the pursuit of *musha shugyō*. During this year, as they
wandered from one province to the other amid an increasingly pacified nation, the old master imparted all that he
knew to his newly found disciple. Already he had given to
Tenzen his precious *Kamewari*, a priceless sword made by
Ichimonji, the famous swordsmith from Bizen. Now he
provided Tenzen with the knowledge that had made it such
an invincible tool in the hands of its previous owner.
Following the duel on the plains of Kogane, he made it clear
that he was preparing to abandon the life of a warrior. He
was looking for a propitious moment when he could take
the tonsure, as he wanted to spend his last days on earth in
meditative seclusion, as the great Jion had done exactly two
centuries earlier.

Ittōsai's moment came in the spring of 1592, when he and Tenzen were invited to Edo castle to give a demonstration of their skills to Ieyasu and his son Hidetada.

It seems that the warlord was impressed with Tenzen's performance, for he made him his personal fencing partner. Along with his new position as official fencing instructor, Tenzen was raised to the rank of *gokenin*, one of Ieyasu's direct vassals. As such he received a stipend of three hundred *koku*, a handsome remuneration by the standards of the late sixteenth century. To mark this remarkable turn in his life Tenzen changed his name to Ono Jirōemon Tadaaki, taking the former from his mother, who was a descendant of the Ono clan. It was Ieyasu's son who gave Tenzen his third name, Tadaaki, the first character of which corresponded with the second character in Hidetada's name. He had done so in recognition for Tenzen's formidable mastery of spear fighting, an art which the latter had learned from the Hōjō warriors during the defense of Ajiro castle.

Tokugawa Hidetada,
who gave Tanzen
his third name

During the following years Ono Tadaaki married. By the time his wife was expecting children, they had moved from Hongō to Surugadai. Situated at the center of the metropolis, between the northern moat of Edo castle and the Kanda River, the Surugadai district had been designated by Ieyasu as the living quarters for his retainers from Suruga. As the years passed, Tadaaki's fame spread, and so did his wealth. By the end of the century, the stipend of the Ono clan had risen to eight hundred *koku*. Tadaaki passed on the tradition of Ittō-ryū to his son, Tadatsune, who went on to become the fencing partner of Ieyasu's grandson, Iemitsu.

Yet even while Tadaaki and his offspring were basking in the glory that came with their position, already during Tadaaki's life the prestige of the Ittō-ryū was eclipsed by a totally different school of fencing. That school of fencing hailed from the other side of the country, from Yamato, the very province from which Tadaaki's distant ancestors had been driven long, long ago.

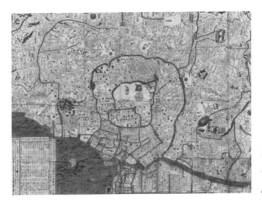

Old map of Edo, with Edo castle at its center

Surugadai, living quarters of the Suruga retainers

It must have been a source of considerable irritation to the members of the proud Ono clan that the tradition of fencing now overshadowing their own was still young when compared to the two-centuries-old tradition of the Ittō-ryū. Founded only a few decades earlier, the school was known as the Yagyū Shinkage-ryū.

Tadaaki was not unfamiliar with this school of fencing. Long before he set forth on his first *musha shugyō*, he had heard of its existence and in the course of his wanderings he had learned a great deal more. Kanemaki Jisai, who had visited the province of Yamato and had instructed the Yagyū in the Toda-ryū, had told him how the Shinkage-ryū had its roots in Aisu Ikkō's Kage-ryū, that it had been founded by a swordsman from Kōzuke, and that the latter had been a retainer of Nagano Narimasa, the former lord of Minowa castle. Narimasa's son, he knew, had fallen in 1567, when Takeda Shingen had laid siege of the castle following Narimasa's death. He had learned more about this episode while reading the first tentative drafts of Obata Kagenori's *Kōyō gunkan*, which described how, following the castle's capture, Shingen had taken into his service over two hundred horsemen who had served Narimori, and that:

> Among them was one Kamiizumi Ise no Kami, who was highly famed for his valor and ability in military matters. He pleaded with Shingen for permission to retire. This was because he had studied the school of swordsmanship known as the Aisu Kage-ryū, improved on it, and created what he called the Shinkage-ryū. He now wished to improve that style of swordsmanship by a journey throughout the provinces to test and further his skill as a swordsman.

On those travels Kamiizumi Ise no Kami had stayed at the castle of the chieftain Yagyū Sekishūsai Muneyoshi. Muneyoshi had studied the Shinkage-ryū of his guest and developed his own style, the Yagyū Shinkage-ryū. That tradition had been inherited by his son, and it was the exploits of the latter, Yagyū Tajima no Kami Munenori, that caused the star of the Yagyū Shinkage-ryū to rise the highest in the firmament of medieval swordsmanship.

PRINCIPAL CHARACTERS IN THIS CHAPTER

Akechi Mitsuhide:	Vassal of Oda Nobunaga who turned against his former lord and assassinated him at the Honnō temple.
Asai Nagamasa:	Lord of Odani castle and ally of Asakura Yoshikage in their attempts to resist Oda Nobunaga's drive toward central control.
Asakura Kageaki:	Lord of Iyama castle, who gave refuge to his relative Asakura Yoshikage with the intent to deliver him into the hands of Toyotomi Hideyoshi.
Asakura Kagetake:	General who led the Asakura forces in the disastrous Battle of Ane River.
Asakura Takakage:	Chieftain of the Asakura clan during the middle of the fifteenth century who built Ichijōdani castle and established the clan's famous martial traditions.
Asakura Yoshikage:	Chieftain of the Asakura clan during Itō Ittōsai's stay at Ichijōdani castle.
Ashikaga Mochiuji:	*Kantō kubō* who fell out with his deputies from among the powerful Uesugi clan and was eventually forced to commit suicide.
Ashikaga Yoshiaki:	Fifteenth Muromachi shogun, taken into protection by Asakura Yoshikage following the assassination of his brother, Yoshiteru, and later the protégé of Oda Nobunaga in the latter's quest for centralized control.
Ashikaga Yoshiaki:	Former monk who returned to secular life in the hope of installing himself as the new *kantō kubō*.

FAMOUS JAPANESE SWORDSMEN

Ashikaga Yoshiteru: Thirteenth Muromachi shogun, who was assassinated by Matsunaga Hisahide.

Chūjō Nagahide: Pupil of the great Nenami Jion and founder of the Chūjō school of fencing.

Hōjō Tsunashige: Stepbrother of Hōjō Ujitsuna who launched a seaborne assault against the Satomi territories across the Uraga Straits.

Hōjō Ujimasa: Successor to Hōjō Ujitsuna, who was able to renew his clan's efforts to subdue the Bōsō Peninsula by signing a pact with their archenemy Takeda Shingen.

Hōjō Ujitsuna: Chieftain of the Hōjō clan who sought to capitalize on the contest for the Satomi leadership to bring the Bōsō peninsula under his control.

Itō Ittōsai: Founder of the Ittō school of fencing, who engaged with Ono Tadaaki in duel at Isumi, later accepted him as his pupil, and then as his successor following Tadaaki's duel with Zenki on their pilgrimage to Nenami Jion's place of birth.

Kanemaki Jisai: Fellow pupil of Itō Ittōsai, who escaped into Mino together with Itō Ittōsai and Toda Shigemasa prior to the fall of Ichijōdani castle and taught Ono Tadaaki the rudiments of the Toda school of fencing during their stay at Ajiro castle.

Kisō Jingō: Local clan leader allied to Satomi Yoshitoyo, who made battle with the Mikogami in the Battle of Inukake.

Kitabatake Tomonori: Governor of Ise and known for his pursuit of the dual way of *bunbu ryōdō*.

Kosaka Masanobu:	Lord of Kaizu castle and vassal of Takeda Shingen.
Kotōda Toshinao:	Lord of Ajiro castle, who called in the help of Toki Yoriharu against the naval threat of the belligerent Satomi Yoshiyasu.
Mariyatsu Nobutaka:	Member of the the Takeda clan who defected to the side of the Hōjō, by whom he was rewarded with the control over Mariyatsu castle.
Mariyatsu Nobuyasu:	Fierce enemy of the Hōjō who gave refuge to Satomi Yoshitoyo during the latter's contest with his cousin.
Masaki Michitsuna:	A naval expert descendant from the Miura clan and an ally to Satomi Sanetaka in the contest for the Satomi leadership.
Masaki Tokishige:	Son of Masaki Michitsuna and lord of Ōtaki castle.
Masaki Tokitada:	Brother of Masaki Tokishige and lord of Katsura castle.
Masaki Yoritada:	Lord of Katsura castle who attacked Obama castle during Yarita Katsutada's absence and then proceeded to lay siege to Mangi castle.
Matsunaga Hisahide:	Warlord from Yamato who assassinated shogun Ashikaga Yoshiteru.
Mikogami Shōzō:	Ono Tadaaki's grandfather, who entered the service of the Toki clan.
Mikogami Tosa:	Ono Tadaaki's father, who died in the defense of Mangi castle.
Miura Tokitaka:	Warlord from the Miura Peninsula, whose demise boosted the naval power of the Satomi and the Hōjō.

Nenami Jion:	Founder of the Nen school of fencing and teacher to Chūjō Nagahide, who passed his style of fencing on to Toda Nagaie, the founder of the Toda school of fencing.
Nitta Yoshisada:	Leader of the Loyalist campaign.
Obata Kagenori:	Son of Obata Masamori and chief author and compiler of *Kōyō gunkan*, who met with Ono Tadaaki at Hizaori and helped him attain a position at the office of Edo's *machi bugyō*.
Obata Masamori:	Garrison commander of Kaizu castle and founder of the Kōshū school of warfare.
Oda Nobunaga:	Warlord from Owari, and the first of Japan's three great unifiers.
Sakai Tadatsugu:	General who led one of Tokugawa Ieyasu's battalions to face those of the Asakura in the Battle of Ane River.
Sakuhime:	Sister of Hōjō Ujimasa, who was married off to Satomi Yoshiyori to improve relations between the two clans.
Satomi Sanetaka:	Brother of Satomi Yoshimichi who, following the death of his brother, vied for leadership of the Satomi clan with his nephew Satomi Yoshitoyo.
Satomi Yoshihiro:	Son and successor to Satomi Yoshitaka.
Satomi Yoshimichi:	Grandson of Satomi Yoshizane and the last patriarch to rule over an undivided Satomi clan.
Satomi Yoshitaka:	Son of Satomi Sanetaka, who slew his cousin Yoshitoyo in the Battle of Inukake and installed himself as the new Satomi chieftain with the help of the Hōjō.

Satomi Yoshitoshi:	Founder of the Satomi clan in Kōzuke.
Satomi Yoshitoyo:	Oldest son of Satomi Yoshimichi, who vied for leadership over the Satomi clan with his uncle Satomi Sanetaka.
Satomi Yoshiyasu:	Son and successor to Satomi Yoshiyori, who discarded his father's policy of appeasement by breaking the fragile truce with the Hōjō.
Satomi Yoshiyori:	Brother and successor to Satomi Yoshihiro, who embarked on a policy of appeasement with the Hōjō.
Satomi Yoshizane:	Chieftain of the Satomi who was forced to flee from his domains in Kōzuke and settle in the Bōsō Peninsula.
Takeda Katsuyori:	Son and successor to Takeda Shingen, who was hunted down by Oda Nobunaga's vassal and finally committed suicide on Mount Tenmoku.
Takeda Shingen:	Warlord from Kai and main rival of Hōjō Ujitsuna.
Tōchi Ōtoshi:	Ono Tadaaki's great grandfather, who fled to the Bōsō Peninsula with his lord Satomi Yoshizane following the fall of Yūki castle and founded the Mikogami clan.
Toda Ippō:	The swordsman who defeated the young Itō Ittōsai in duel and advised him to travel down to Echizen and enter the service of the Asakura clan.
Toda Kageie:	Son of Toda Nagaie.
Toda Kagemasa:	Son of Toda Kageie.
Toda Nagaie:	Pupil of Chūjō Nagahide and founder of the Toda school of fencing.

Toda Seigen: Son of Toda Kageie and chief propagator of the Toda school of fencing.

Toda Shigemasa: Star pupil and adoptive son of Toda Kagemasa, who escaped into Mino together with Itō Ittōsai and Kanemaki Jisai prior to the fall of Ichijōdani castle.

Toki Tameyori: Lord of the Mikogami clan and ally to Satomi Sanetaka and the latter's son, Yoshitaka, in the contest for the Satomi leadership.

Toki Yoriharu: Son and successor to Toki Tameyori.

Tokugawa Hidetada: Son of Tokugawa Ieyasu from whom Ono Tadaaki received the first character of his given name after he was appointed as Hidetada's fencing instructor.

Tokugawa Ieyasu: Warlord from Mikawa, third of Japan's three great unifiers.

Toyotomi Hideyoshi: Warlord from Owari, second of Japan's three great unifiers.

Uesugi Kenshin: Warlord from Echigo and rival of Hōjō Ujitsuna who came to the rescue of Satomi Yoshitaka.

Yamazaki Yoshiie: Vassal of Asakura Yoshikage who helped the latter in his unsuccessful and last attempt to resist Oda Nobunaga.

Yarita Katsutada: Lord of Obama castle and vassal of Toki Yoriharu, who led the naval expedition to assist Kotōda Toshinao at Ajiro castle against the threat of the belligerent Satomi Yoshiyasu.

YAGYŪ TAJIMA NO KAMI MUNENORI

柳生但馬守宗則

Genki 2–Shōhō 3
(1571–1648)

Among the many schools of fencing that have survived the centuries, the Shinkage school stands out for its continuity. Throughout the Edo Period (1600–1867) the heritage of Kamiizumi Ise no Kami Nobutsuna remained at the forefront of martial life. One of the secrets behind the success of the Shinkage-ryū is undoubtedly its close association with the Yagyū clan. For over four centuries this ancient clan from the hills around Nara, which traces its ancestry back to the late ninth century, has guarded over Nobutsuna's intellectual heritage and seen to it that its tenets and techniques have remained unsullied by the changing moods of time.

Iizasa Chōisai Ienao, founder of the Shintō-ryū

It was different for many of the other schools brought forth in the fourteenth, fifteenth, and sixteenth centuries, many of which remained within the same clan for only a few generations, or even less. Iizasa Chōisai Ienao's famous Shintō school of fencing, for instance, was passed on to Matsumoto Masanobu, who passed it on to Tsukahara Tosa no Yasumoto, who in turn passed it on to his adoptive son, Tsukahara Shinsaemon Tosa no Kami, alias Tsukahara Bokuden, one of the great swordsmen of the sixteenth century. The same was true for Nenami Okuyama Jion's school of fencing. If anything, the survival of his Nen-ryū was even more precarious. Where the practitioners of the Shintō-ryū had chiefly hailed from the provinces of Shimōsa and Hitachi, those of the Nen-ryū all hailed from different parts of the country, Jion from Shimōsa, Chūjō Nagahide from Mikawa, Toda Nagaie from Echizen, Itō Ittōsai Kagehisa from Itō, and Mikogami Tenzen from the province of Kazusa.

The transmission of a school of fencing from one generation to another, then, was fraught with dangers. And while
the greatest danger lay in the lack of disciples, or *deshi*, even
a swordsman blessed with a great number of followers could
never be sure that his life's work would outlive him. Only
when a *deshi* remained with his master for a protracted
period, usually a period of several years, could a master find
the patience, trust, and time to impart the full scope of his
teachings. This had been the case when Mikogami Tenzen
had joined Itō Ittōsai on his *musha shugyō*, and it had been
the case when Nobutsuna had relied on the hospitality of
Yagyū Muneyoshi after the fall of Minowa castle. The
majority of such encounters, however, were of a fleeting
nature, disrupted by an unexpected turn of events, and often
too brief for a master swordsman to impart the full weight
of his knowledge. Tenzen's encounter with Kanemaki Jisai
had been such an example. Had Tenzen not subsequently
gone up to Edo, to be hired by Obata Kagenori and revisited

*Tsukahara Bokuden, one of the great
swordsmen of the 16th century*

129

by his one-time dueling partner, it is unlikely that Jion's heritage would have survived the way it did. Such fortune, however, was rare. More often a style of fencing died with its founder—on the field of battle, in a duel, or due to a lack of *deshi*. It is a testament to the quality of the techniques of Chōisai's Shintō-ryū and Jion's Ittō-ryū that they overcame these hurdles to form the three main schools of fencing of the Edo period alongside Kamiizumi's Shinkage-ryū.

Nobutsuna's Shinkage-ryū never suffered from such impediments, as his intellectual heritage only had to make this arduous transition once. Following his protracted stay at Yagyū castle during the 1560s, the transmission of his teachings remained the prerogative of the Yagyū clan. And while the Shinkage-ryū spawned a myriad of new and diverging schools, it was the Yagyū clan that continued to practice and teach the same style of fencing throughout the centuries that followed. From the moment Nobutsuna bestowed on Yagyū Muneyoshi a *mokuroku*, a written inventory of the

Kamiizumi Nobutsuna, founder of the Shinkage-ryū

techniques and tenets of the Shinkage-ryū (the medieval equivalent of a teaching license), the document and the school it represents, has been passed down to each successive Yagyū generation, right down to today. It was this remarkable continuity that secured the success of the Yagyū Shinkage school of fencing. Yet the foundation for endurance of the Yagyū clan itself was laid by Muneyoshi's son. Had it not been for the brilliant career of Yagyū Munenori it is unlikely that Nobutsuna's heritage would have survived the ravishes of time the way it did.

Yagyū Munenori was born in 1571. He had four older brothers—Yoshikatsu, Yoshihide, Munetaka, and Muneaki. Being the youngest, Munenori was destined to spend his early youth in relative idleness, practicing the art of fencing with his brothers and making votive offerings at the local shrine for the repose of his ancestors' souls. To the clan, however, the birth of another boy was the symbol of renewed hope, for the Yagyū at this time were struggling hard to recover from a string of misfortunes.

Those misfortunes had begun in 1544, when the Yagyū domains were overrun by the Tsutsui, a clan from the Nara basin. Munenori's grandfather had resisted their expansion, but paid for his bravery with the loss of Yagyū castle. Eventually he submitted and set about to rebuild the stronghold. Sixteen years later, the world of the Yagyū had been turned upside down again. The year was 1560, when the Tsutsui were subdued by the Miyoshi, who hailed from the

Miyoshi Chōkei

province of Awa on the island of Shikoku. Again the Yagyū were forced to adjust to a new overlord, the influential Miyoshi Chōkei, in order to survive. While a warlord in the typical mold of his time, Chōkei was an upright man, widely respected for his administrative talents, and for a while the Yagyū accepted their fate with resignation. This changed in 1564, when Miyoshi Chōkei was succeeded by Matsunaga Hisahide, a one-time tea merchant from Kyoto, who had insinuated himself into the position of Chōkei's senior counselor and succeeded him by poisoning his rightful heir. So, at least, went the rumors—rumors that were readily accepted as fact when, within only a year of his succession as chieftain, Hisahide had the thirteenth shogun of the Muromachi Bakufu, Ashikaga Yoshiteru, assassinated, along with his wife and mother. That assassination had forced Yoshiteru's younger brother, Yoshiaki, to fall back on the military clout of Oda Nobunaga, giving the latter, in turn, a pretext to seize the capital.

For the Yagyū clan Nobunaga's arrival in the capital was welcome news. With each year Hisahide's behavior had become more erratic. At first he had been kept in check by his brother, Nagayori, the vice-governor of Tanba province. In every way the opposite of his brother, Nagayori was a warrior of great moral stature, who was respected by the Miyoshi clan. Indeed, it was more out of respect for his brother than for any of his qualities that the Miyoshi had acquiesced to Hisahide's chieftaincy. Thus it came as no surprise to the Yagyū that, when Nagayori died in battle in 1565, the majority of the Miyoshi clan fell out with their new leader and launched a large-scale campaign to recapture the strongholds that he had subdued on their behalf a few years earlier. The first castle to fall into their hands was that of Tsutsui, at the heart of the Nara basin, the clan's traditional power base. Over the next year the fighting spread eastward, toward Nara and Hisahide's headquarters of Tamon castle. The castle stood at a stone's throw from the famous

Matsunaga Hisahide

133

Daibutsuden, the great hall on the premises of the Tōdai monastery. For more than eight centuries the wooden structure had housed a forty-eight-foot-tall bronze Buddha that attracted pilgrims from the far corners of the country. Part of the Miyoshi troops had taken up quarters in and around the premises of the venerated building. Untrammelled by conscience, Hisahide had ordered his men to open fire on the building. The Miyoshi troops were scarcely harmed, but the roof of the building went up in flames, causing the top part of the statue to melt away. The string of depredations by their new overlord eventually forced the Yagyū to go into hiding among the Yoshino Mountains.

When the Yagyū clan went into hiding, they were accompanied by Kamiizumi Ise no Kami Nobutsuna. The great swordsman from Kōzuke had arrived in Yamato in the fall

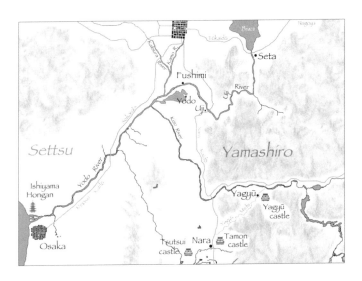

Hōzōin Kakuzenbō In'ei, chief abbot of the Kōfuku monastery

of 1567. He had been on a *musha shugyō*, in the company of two other swordsmen, Jingo Muneharu and Hikida Bungorō, two trusted vassals with whom he had survived the siege of Minowa castle. He and the Yagyū chieftain had met at a fencing contest at the Kōfuku monastery. The contest had been organized by Hōzōin Kakuzenbō In'ei, chief abbot of the monastery and founder of the Hōzōin school of spear fighting. In'ei introduced the two swordsmen. Muneyoshi and Bungorō engaged in a *taryū shiai*, and when Muneyoshi lost he had invited the three swordsmen to come and stay at Yagyū castle. Over the next years they had immersed themselves in their studies, Nobutsuna writing long tracts on the Shinkage-ryū, Muneyoshi absorbing from his new-found teacher all that he could about this new and exhilarating school of fencing. Meanwhile they anxiously followed events, pinning their hopes on the day when forces larger than they could ever hope to muster would turn things in their favor and enable them to reemerge from their

135

self-imposed exile. That day arrived on November 9, 1568, when Oda Nobunaga entered Kyoto in full panoply.

Nobunaga had closely followed the actions of Yamato's warlords, even before marching on the capital. He had denounced their senseless bellicosity, yet he was most critical of Hisahide. Discussing the matter with his ally Ieyasu, he had observed that Hisahide was a man of whom they should be extremely wary, as he had "gained notoriety in this world for three crimes." The first was the assassination of the rightful Miyoshi heir. The second the assassination of the shogun. The third the destruction of the Great Buddha of the Tōdai monastery. Such men belonged to a bygone era, an era in which the guiding principle in life was the dictum of *gekokujō*. How different it was with his own ambitions. His motto, carved into his seal of state for all to read, was *tenka fubu*, to "rule the whole country by force." He was well on his way to achieving that aim, and having just subdued the strategic province of Mino, he was eager to turn his attention to the subjugation of the Home Provinces and lay the foundation for a unified Japan. Yet despite his vexation at Hisahide's outrages, his chief concerns still lay with the *sōhei* of the Tendai and Ikkō sects, who had their headquarters at the Ishiyama Hongan monastery near Osaka. And thus, to deal with the lesser threat from the local warlords, he had put a force of some ten thousand troops under the command of Sakuma Nobumori, an old vassal from Harima province, who had once served his father.

Nobumori marched into Yamato in the autumn of 1568. The Miyoshi resisted. They had thus far held the upper hand in the conflict, and were eager to hold on to what they had gained. But they were no match for Nobumori's well-organized troops, armed as the latter were with lethal *teppō*. One by one they had to abandon the castles they had recaptured from Hisahide, until, by the end of 1569, they had been forced to flee across the Inland Sea, back to their old domains on the island of Shikoku.

The shrewd Hisahide played his cards differently. Even before Nobumori had crossed the Kizu River he had begun to ply Nobunaga with costly gifts of exquisite Chinaware and coveted tea utensils. Never a man to turn down the fawning of a sycophant, Nobunaga responded to the overtures. In spite of his cautious words to his ally Ieyasu, he now decided to grant Hisahide control over the province of Yamato on the condition that he grant amnesty to other local clans and refrain from forging liaisons with those who opposed the drive toward unification. Hisahide was quick to comply with Nobunaga's demands. He moved back into his

The beautiful Kizu River

old headquarters of Tamon castle, from where he sent missives to those with whom he had been at loggerheads. It is doubtful whether the Yagyū would have complied with Hisahide's request had not Nobunaga himself dispatched a missive to the Yagyū clan (as well as many other smaller clans in the region) encouraging them to place themselves under Hisahide's rule, and promising them the necessary financial and military aid if they had to fight on his behalf. Nobunaga's motives in doing so were clear enough. His objective was to secure the capital, whatever the costs, and the ruin of one or more small clans to achieve that objective was a small price to pay. For the Yagyū clan, however, there were few other options, and thus, in the first months of 1670, they came out of hiding and Yagyū Muneyoshi resumed his rightful place as lord of Yagyū castle.

It had been not long after their return to Yagyū castle that Muneyoshi's wife again became pregnant. And while the prospect of a new child brought new happiness to the Yagyū,

*The gate to
Yagyū castle*

there were many worries, too. The Yagyū estate at this point in time was only a fraction of what it had once been. The Yagyū had to live from the little that their estate brought in, which was far too little to support them, their parents, and their ten children. The older of their six daughters had been married off or promised to the sons of neighboring chieftains, while one of their sons had already taken the tonsure and entered one of Nara's many monasteries. It seemed inevitable that, as soon as the new child came of age, it would share the fate of its brothers or sisters. Yet, as so often in life, unforeseen events caused the unborn child to tread a path quite different from the one its parents had foreseen.

It was in the summer of 1570, not more than a few months after the Yagyū clan had returned to Yagyū castle, that the fate of the yet unborn Munenori was decided by the actions of a clan that had once ruled supreme in the province of Yamato. In that year, the once powerful Tsutsui clan rose against Matsunaga Hisahide. Following their expulsion from the family stronghold of Tsutsui castle they had fallen back on Katsuragi castle, along the border with Kawachi province, from where they held on tenaciously to their last remaining foothold in their former province. They were led by the twenty-year-old Tsutsui Junkei, who had just laid to rest his uncle and patron, Tsutsui Junsei.

Since the death of Junkei's father, his uncle had worked tirelessly to strengthen the position of his clan, but he had not had the resources to resist the combined threat of

Matsunaga-Miyoshi alliance, and when he died in exile in Sakai, he had done so a broken and disillusioned man.

Junkei had lost many of those close to him in the atrocities that attended Hisahide's rise to power. Only the year before, the daughter and son of two of his close vassals had become the youngest victims of Hisahide's abominations, when at a gruesome festival celebrating his capture of Ido castle, the youths had been impaled alive and put on display outside the castle walls. The act was all the more unbearable as both youngsters had been sent as hostages in order to placate Nobunaga's new representative in the region. Junkei was not the only one to hate Hisahide with a vengeance. Many of the smaller chieftains in the region had also come to loathe Hisahide's rule, and were quick to submit to their former overlord. Hisahide's ability to unite his opponents was remarkable, for even the Miyoshi, once such sworn enemies of the Tsutsui, now joined the fray and eagerly conspired in Junkei's plans to overthrow the hated tyrant.

Those plans were put into action in the summer of 1670, when, on July 25, Junkei led a force of some five hundred men into Yamato province and recaptured Tōchi castle, the home of Ono Tadaaki's distant relatives, near the town of Kashihara. From there they marched northward, toward Nara and Hisahide's headquarters of Tamon castle, setting fire to large parts of the town and ensconcing themselves in the grounds of the Kōninji, an ancient temple on the crest of Takahi hill, on the town's southern outskirts.

The assault had taken Hisahide by surprise. His obligations toward his new ally had drawn his attention elsewhere,

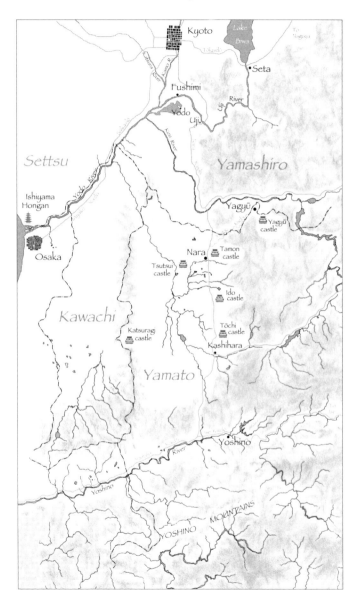

Tsutsui Junkei, eager to regain what had been taken from his father

required as he was to assist Nobunaga in the defense of the Home Provinces. This was a tall order, for even Nobunaga was hard pressed at this time.

By now Nobunaga not only had to deal with the belligerent Ikkō sectarians, but also the powerful Miyoshi, who had signed a pact with the sectarians and landed in force near the Ishiyama Hongan temple. From there they had marched into Yamashiro and Kawachi to recapture their former strongholds. Then they headed for Kyoto, where, reinforced by a garrison of some three thousand Hongan musketeers, they began to attack Nobunaga's troops, causing a great number of casualties. The situation grew even more threatening when the Asai and Asakura clans, having recovered from their first defeat at Ane River, were joined by *sōhei* from the Enryaku monastery of Mount Hiei and began to stir up trouble once more in Mino. The combined effect of these various assaults from different corners forced Nobunaga to shorten his line and concentrate on the defense of the capital and his headquarters of Gifu castle, leaving Hisahide and other local allied chieftains to deal with the Miyoshi elsewhere. Complying with Nobunaga's orders, Hisahide had led a force of close to two thousand across the border with Kawachi to engage in battle with the Miyoshi at Tennōji, near Osaka. It was this temporary absence that gave Junkei the opportunity to slip back into Yamato. Alarmed by the swiftness with which the Tsutsui had been able to encroach on his home base he ordered one of his chief commanders, Takeuchi Hidekatsu, to return to Nara and secure his headquarters of from Junkei's onslaught.

The very first thing Hidekatsu did on his return to Tamon castle, on August 23, was to send missives to allied local chieftains, among them Yagyū Muneyoshi. They were ordered to mobilize their menfolk and immediately come up to Nara. There they were to put themselves under the command of the Nakanobō clan and launch an attack on the Tsutsui positions that same day. It was a shrewd move by the seasoned commander. The mansion of the Nakanobō was located in Tsubai, on Nara's southern outskirts, the area that had been most affected by the skirmishes. The Yagyū were related to the Nakanobō, and he knew that they would feel obliged to fight for the Nakanobō even while, like the Nakanobō, they might despise Hisahide. Perhaps he even shared their sentiments, for within a year, he himself, too, was to fall out of favor with his master. He, too, would seek to mollify his master in vain by offering his son as hostage, and he, too, would eventually be forced to commit ritual suicide and become a victim of Hisahide's evil whims.

As Hidekatsu had anticipated, his appeal to the Yagyū had not fallen on deaf ears, The connection between the Yagyū and Nakanobō went all the way back to the beginning of the fourteenth century, to the events leading up to the Kenmu Restoration, when the Yagyū clan was led by Yagyū Nagayoshi. It had been in 1331, in the first year of the Genkō era, that emperor Go-Daigo left the comforts of the Kazan palace in Kyoto behind in his first bid to restore to his throne the powers it had originally enjoyed. He had taken up residence at the Kasagi temple, an old temple of the Shingon sect amid the Kasagi Mountains. From there he issued an edict, calling on all warrior chieftains loyal to the throne to support his cause and overthrow the Kamakura Bakufu. Yagyū Nagayoshi had been the first chieftain to respond to the call to arms. The Yagyū clan had long been at logger-heads with the regime in far-away Kamakura, while Kasagi temple was situated along the Kizu River, less than a mile north of their estate. He had sent his brother, Yoshitaka, to

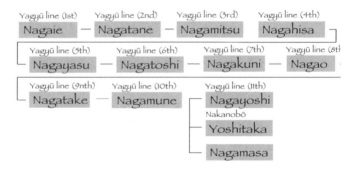

Yagyū clan lineage, from Nagaie, to Nagayoshi and (Nakanobō) Yoshitaka

144

Kasagi temple, inextricably linked to the history of the Yagyū clan

guard the temple with all the troops they could muster. The Genkō Rebellion came to nothing. Go-Daigo was sent into exile on Oki island, and the Yagyū clan lost its possessions. Two years later, however, Go-Daigo escaped. That escape had led to Nitta Yoshisada's revolt, the overthrow of the Kamakura Bakufu, and the Kenmu Restoration. In reward for their valiant service Go-Daigo rewarded Yoshitaka by granting him the name of Nakanobō, "monk among monks," and restoring to his clan the lands that had belonged to it since time immemorial. Yoshitaka had remained in the emperor's service and left Nagayoshi to manage the Yagyū estates, as he had done during the years prior to the outbreak of the Genkō Rebellion.

When the messenger arrived at Yagyū castle in the early hours of the morning, Muneyoshi had scrambled all the men he could muster and headed straight for Nara. His eldest son, Yoshikatsu, was nineteen at the time and, having entreated his father, he was allowed to join them.

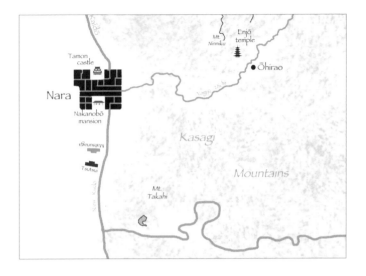

The warriors of the Yagyū and Nakanobō clans fought hard and bravely that day, united as they were in the knowledge that they were fighting for their very survival. The fighting was concentrated on the southern outskirts of the ancient capital, as it had been over the previous days. Rallying their troops at their old mansion in Tsubai, the Nakanobō had launched a counter-offensive to drive the Tsutsui out. But when Muneyoshi and his son rode out from Tsubai to charge the makeshift defenses the Tsutsui had erected along Nara's southern approaches, they soon realized that the forces they were up against were formidable. On his march from Tōchi castle, Junkei had been joined by other disgruntled chieftains, and the small force of five hundred men with which he had set out had meanwhile swollen to a few thousand. Among them were also *sōhei* from Negoro and Kii, many of them armed with the fearsome muskets. Some of Hidekatsu's troops, too, were armed with muskets, but the Yagyū, who had spent the previous years in hiding, were still fighting in the traditional way. Their superior mastery of the sword still made them a force to be reckoned with, but only when fighting at close quarters.

In spite of these overwhelming odds the Yagyū and Nakanobō warriors pressed on. It seemed that history was repeating itself, for again they were fighting side by side, and again they seemed to be fighting a losing battle. After a day of intense fighting they managed to evict the Tsutsui from their makeshift defenses and drive them out of town, back to their stronghold on Mount Takahi. Strategically, it was a victory of sorts, but in sheer numbers the Matsunaga forces had suffered a crushing defeat. Few of their ranks had escaped unharmed, nor had the Yagyū been spared that day. During one of the charges Yoshikatsu had been hit in the back by a bullet, and thrown off his horse by the impact.

Kōnin temple with Mount Takahi in the background

147

Though lodged in his back, the bullet had not made a large wound, and all seemed well when the young man began to move. The truth only dawned on Muneyoshi when he goaded his son to get back on his horse. Whether it was the damage wrought by the bullet or the way he had fallen, the young warrior was unable to rise. The nerves in his spine had been severed and he was crippled from the waist down.

Yoshikatsu's incapacitation proved a profound setback to the prospects of the Yagyū clan. At barely nineteen he was Muneyoshi's oldest son, and as such he was expected to bear a large part of the burden in the management and defense of the Yagyū estate and to succeed his father in the not too distant future. Now that future suddenly seemed a bleak one. None of Yoshikatsu's younger brothers were of an age where they could take his position. Two of them, Yoshihide and Munetaka, had by now taken the tonsure, assumed the spiritual names of Kyūsai and Tokusai, and entered one of Nara's monasteries. This left Muneyoshi with just Muneaki, who had turned five that year.

It was an impossible situation for the aging Muneyoshi. Fighting on behalf of Hisahide in 1566, he, too, had been wounded, his left hand pierced by an arrow. The wound had healed, but he lost much of the strength of his grip. The handicap did not affect him when fighting on horseback, when one usually brandished a sword in one hand, but on foot, when the sword was held with both hands, it considerably diminished his ability to engage in man-to-man combat.

For a warrior who prided himself on his swordsmanship it was a serious handicap—one that had contributed to his defeat at the hands of Kamiizumi Nobutsuna's disciple, Hikida Bungorō, with whom he engaged in a duel at the Kōfuku monastery the following year. Now, however, things were far more serious. With an aging father, a number of daughters, a five-year-old infant, a crippled son to care for, and his wife pregnant with yet another child, the continuity of his clan was in serious jeopardy. And thus Muneyoshi and his family set out along along the Yagyū Michi, the old road that connected Yagyū village with the temple town of Nara. Eager to stay in the vicinity of their rightful domains they went into hiding in Ōhirao, a small village at the foot of Mount Ninniku, on the hallowed grounds of the famous Enjō temple.

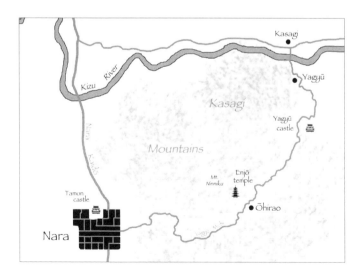

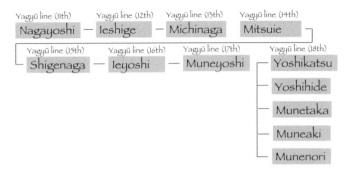

Yagyū clan lineage, from Nagayoshi to Munenori and his four brothers

It was during the first months of their self-imposed exile at Ōhirao that Muneyoshi's wife delivered a healthy son. They named him Matasaemon. When he came of age early in the 1580s Matasaemon received his formal name of Munenori, the first of the two characters with which it was written being derived from the name of from his father, as well as many of his distant ancestors.

A lot had happened in that uncertain decade. In 1573 Nobunaga had ousted the sitting shogun, Ashikaga Yoshiaki from Nijō castle and sent him into exile, thus bringing about the end of the Muromachi Bakufu. He had forged ties with Nobunaga's archrival Takeda Shingen, calling on him to overthrow Nobunaga and restore power to the Bakufu. That year, however, Shingen died, thus removing perhaps the greatest threat to Nobunaga's plan to pacify the country. And while Matsunaga Hisahide, too, had responded to the shogun's call, his well-timed conciliatory gestures had once again saved him from the lion's clutches, and over the next few years he made well his promises by assisting Nobunaga in the siege of the Ishiyama Hongan monastery.

Tsutsui Junkei, meanwhile, had stubbornly persevered in his campaign to evict Hisahide and reclaim his clan's former territories. It was one of those paradoxes of a country in war that Junkei, too, had formed an alliance with Nobunaga, contributing large numbers of musketeers to the battle of Nagashino, but somehow Hisahide had continued to get the better of him. In the year following his march on Nara he managed to recapture the family stronghold of Tsutsui castle, forcing Hisahide to fall back on his old headquarters of Shigisan castle. But Junkei's commitments to Nobunaga in quelling the Ikkō sectarians and Hisahide's position of power kept him from gaining much territory. What he desperately needed was an opportunity to wrest from Hisahide the trust that he so undeservedly enjoyed.

That opportunity came toward the end 1576, when one of Junkei's spies at Tamon castle informed him that Hisahide

Ikkō sectarians

151

had entered into secret negotiations with none other than Uesugi Kenshin. Kenshin, too, had long had his sights on the capital, but thus far his archrival, Takeda Shingen, had kept him pinned down in the north. With Shingen's death that barrier was removed, and early in 1576, he began to approach Nobunaga's chief rivals in the Home Provinces in the hope of forming an alliance. It was not long before Nobunaga was informed of Hisahide's treachery, and his response was exactly as Junkei had hoped. He immediately stripped Hisahide of his governorship, bestowing it instead on Junkei. Hisahide's response was by now predictable. Offended by Nobunaga's "betrayal," and aware that he now faced the Tsutsui and their allies alone, he reconciled himself with the Miyoshi, thus hoping to counter by force what he had failed to avoid by subterfuge. It was not enough, for one of those allies now included Nobunaga. In the summer of 1577, Junkei, his allies, and a large contingent under the command of Nobunaga's eldest son, Nobutada, converged

Oda Nobutada, the warrior who brought Matsunaga Hisahide to heel

*Shigisan castle,
headquarters of
the notorious
Matsunaga
Hisahide*

on Shigisan castle. Seeing that his game was up, Hisahide withdrew to the main tower of his castle and committed suicide by detonating a cast-iron tea kettle filled with gunpowder. It was the end of an ignominious career, a career that had begun ten years earlier with the destruction of the Hall of the Great Buddha.

Hisahide's death brought little relief to the smaller chieftains of Yamato province. In the summer of 1580, following the surrender of the Ishiyama Hongan monastery after a decade of almost uninterrupted fighting, Nobunaga issued a decree that all the castles and fortifications in the surrounding provinces of Settsu, Kawachi, and Yamato were to be demolished forthwith. Even major castles such as those of Tamon and Shigisan were to be destroyed. Nobunaga's orders were executed with such rigor and at such pace that by the fall of the next year almost all of the castles littering the Yamato landscape were laid in ruins. Only Junkei, as Nobunaga's appointed representative in Yamato, was allowed to maintain a castle, a right on which he capitalized in the very same year of Nobunaga's decree, when he began construction of a vast castle at Kōriyama, situated southwest of Nara at the center of the Nara Basin.

Nobunaga's decree was a drastic measure brought forth by an age of dramatic events. In the greater scheme of things it was an act that immediately bore fruit. Already by 1581, when most of the castles in Yamato had been laid in ruins, the monk Eishun, abbot of the Tamon monastery in Nara, recorded in his *Tamon-in nikki* the effect of Nobunaga's policies, when he observed that "not a single battle has upset the tranquillity that has descended on the region following the fall of the Ishiyama Hongan monastery." It seemed that Nobunaga's ruthless persecution of the Ikkō sectarians that had followed the fall of the Nagashima, inhuman though it had been, had had the desired effect and that at long last the peace and prosperity the fertile region had once known would again be allowed to flourish. Yet the same measures that were so beneficial to the region's common dwellers, the countryside farmers and the town citizens, sounded the death-knell for its many local chieftains.

The Yagyū, too, felt the full brunt of Nobunaga's measure, for their castle had not escaped the notice of Junkei's administrators. In the fall of 1580, having weathered more than two and a half centuries of civil war and a long drawn-out siege by Junkei's ancestors, Yagyū castle, the proud abode of the Yagyū clan, was razed to the ground. Many a chieftain submitted, choosing to become mere retainers in Junkei's army. Others fled across the borders in the hope of

The remains of
Yagyū castle

establishing themselves elsewhere, where Nobunaga's power did not reach. Not so Yagyū Muneyoshi, who could not afford to leave his family behind. His father, Ieyoshi, was now advanced in years, while Munenori, his one able son who was still with him, was still only six years old, far too young to assume any responsibility even in a feudal age. And thus he and his family continued their life of seclusion in the shadow of Mount Ninniku, biding their time.

While these dramatic events were playing out on the plains of the Nara basin, the Yagyū were making the most of their self-imposed exile. It had been during their first period in hiding, between 1567 and 1568 that their guest Kamiizumi Nobutsuna had found the time to write his memoirs and to impart his knowledge of the Shinkage school of fencing to Yagyū Muneyoshi. Though deeply trying, spiritually they had been rewarding times, and in the vacuum of their fugitive existence Muneyoshi had thoroughly absorbed all the tenets and intricacies of this, to him, new and revolutionary school of fencing. Satisfied that he had finally found the man who could pass on his intellectual heritage to posterity, Nobutsuna had granted his disciple a so-called *inka*, a document Buddhist in origin by which a master certified that his pupil had reached maturity in training. It read:

> Since my early youth I have sought to master the arts of swordsmanship and military tactics, exploring the *okugi* of various schools. I meditated and practiced day and night, until the gods enabled me to found the Shinkage-ryū. When I visited Kyoto in my quest to propagate my school of fencing throughout the land I unexpectedly met you, and you were solicitous and sincere in many ways. And while I find it hard to find the right words to express my gratitude, I hereby declare that I have, without any omissions, transmitted to you my full knowledge of this school of fencing and the state of mind its practitioners will achieve.

More than a decade had passed since Nobutsuna had written these words. Muneyoshi was now well into his fifties, and in a world in which few reached old age he was beginning to feel the urge to pass on the intellectual heritage of his great teacher. Nobutsuna had been sixty when he had revealed the *okugi* of the Shinkage-ryū, and now Muneyoshi himself realized that the time had come to take his rightful place in the line of transmission and instill in his son the skills that had led the then shogun Ashikaga Yoshiaki to

Ashikaga Yoshiaki, who raised Nobutsuna to the exalted rank of jūshi-i

raise Nobutsuna to the exalted rank of *jūshi-i*, or Fourth-Level Warrior Follower—an honor bestowed on no other swordsman past or present.

To Muneyoshi's great delight and comfort Munenori proved a fiercely intelligent child, with a natural aptness for learning as well as fighting. Well before the boy had come of age, it was clear to his father that Munenori was destined to become a great swordsmen, while his quick insight and resolute action inspired high hopes for his future as the leader of the Yagyū clan.

Munenori's intellectual inclinations led him to look beyond the immediate needs of the day and contemplate the future. As a child he had had the freedom to travel where his father did not, and on the few occasions that he had visited his brothers in Nara he was reminded of the suffering the centuries of civil strife had inflicted on the populace. He knew that since the Ōnin war the capital had been rebuilt more than once, but in Nara many of the great buildings still

157

The restored Geat Buddha of the Tōdai monastery's Daibutsuden

bore the scars of internecine warfare. The most terrible sight among the many ruins was the ghostly specter of the Daibutsuden. All that remained standing were the charred sections of its walls and the decapitated trunk of the once so magnificent Great Buddha. Whenever the young Munenori set his eyes on the blackened and headless torso, protruding ominously from the palisade of charred woodwork, it seemed to the young man that even the benevolence of the Great Buddha had been exhausted by the constant warring, bringing home to him the vanity of power and the need for peace in a war-torn country. That awareness strengthened the young man in his resolve to turn his martial skills to the good, an aim his father was prone to sum up in the term *katsujinken*, or the "life-giving sword."

For the time being, however, Munenori and his family and all those who dwelled in the Home Provinces were in the grip of epoch-making events, and one of them was Nobunaga's assassination at the hands of Akechi Mitsuhide during his stay at the Honnō temple in Kyoto. The first scraps of news of a disturbance at the Honnō temple had reached the village of Ōhirao toward the middle of May 1582. The reports were at first sketchy, no more than a confusing collection of rumors, but as time drew on the rumors were reinforced with more and more strands of information until the true scale of events and its consequences for the Yamato chieftains became apparent.

It had been early in May 1582, that Oda Nobunaga was sojourning in the capital. He had been making preparations to march for Bitchū, where his chief general, Toyotomi Hideyoshi, was laying siege to Takamatsu castle, a Mōri stronghold. The Mōri, it appeared, were offering fierce opposition, forcing the general to appeal to Nobunaga for reinforcements. Nobunaga had seemed confident of victory over the Mōri, and gone about his preparations with a degree of leisure. On the evening of May 1 he had even found the time to organize a tea ceremony at the Honnō temple, his usual abode when he visited the capital. He had been in high spirits that evening, entertaining his guests with tales from his early youth, and utterly oblivious to the looming threat. By the time he and his guest heard the stampeding of hoofs and the clamour of metal it was already too late. Indomitable as ever, Nobunaga had rushed out, shouting that Mitsuhide would "never succeed," but his retinue was utterly outnumbered and at length he had withdrawn into the burning building and committed suicide.

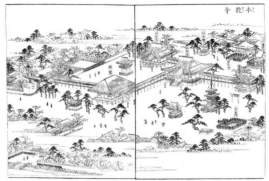

寺能本

The Honnō monastery, site of Nobunaga's assassination

The Honnō Rebellion shocked the nation. Especially in the Home Provinces, where the effects of the Nobunaga's drive toward unification were most palpable, people feared the worst. To Tsutsui Junkei the shock was one of embarrassment, for the ties between the house of Tsutsui and that of Akechi were very close, and it had been through Mitsuhide's personal offices that Nobunaga had granted him the province of Yamato on Matsunaga Hisahide's death. Mitsuhide naturally assumed that he could rely on Junkei's help, as well as on that of a number of other warlords, but the general response had been tepid. Junkei, too, had been reluctant to act. He had raised a small contingent, but when he learned that Hideyoshi had raised camp and begun a forced march toward the capital he balked and stayed put at his new headquarters of Kōriyama castle, unable to make up his mind whether to join Hideyoshi or Mitsuhide.

The showdown between the two antagonists came on June 13, when their forces clashed at the village of Yamazaki.

There, at the strategic narrow of the Hora pass, Mitsuhide awaited the arrival of his enemy Hideyoshi and his ally Junkei. It was less than a day's ride from there to Kōriyama castle, but Junkei's reinforcements never appeared. Aware of Hideyoshi's strength and the other warlord's lukewarm response to Mitsuhide's call to arms, the latter had sent a missive to Himeji castle in Harima, where Hideyoshi was getting ready to march on the capital. In it he pledged his allegiance to the general, vowing not to lift a finger against his troops. In return, for his betrayal—and Mitsuhide's death—Junkei was allowed to hold on to his governorship of Yamato province and continued to reside at Kōriyama castle, where he died following a short illness in 1584.

Leadership over the Tsutsui clan was now assumed by the twenty-three-year-old Sadatsugu. Sadatsugu was not Junkei's

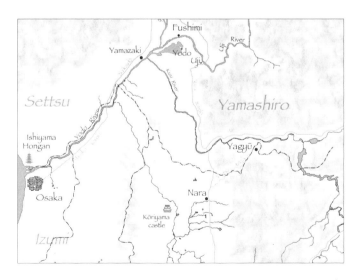

natural heir. He was the oldest son of Tsutsui Junkoku, one of Junkei's uncles, who had helped him to recapture Tōchi castle. After that he continued to support Junkei in his rise to power, but he had done so from behind the scenes, and where Junkei had confronted his enemies, Junkoku had forged ties with potential allies. Junkoku's conciliatory stance had brought about a rapprochement between the Tsutsui and many of the local chieftains from whom they had been alienated over the previous decades—a rapprochement on which Sadatsugu intended to capitalize on his succession, but his plans were upset toward the end of 1585, when he was ordered by Hideyoshi to move his headquarters to Ueno in the neighboring province of Iga. Some of the chieftains who had found peace with the Tsutsui, among them the Nakanobō, continued to serve their new-found lord, and chose to make the move to Iga, Others preferred to keep their domains and chose to serve under the new lord of Kōriyama castle, Hideyoshi's stepbrother Hidenaga.

*Kōriyama castle
as it is today*

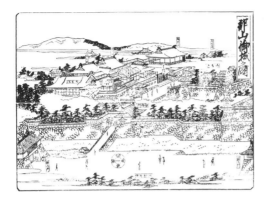

Kōriyama castle in Muneyoshi's day

There were good reasons why Hideyoshi had made his stepbrother the new governor of Yamato. Together with castles in the other Home Provinces, it formed a line of defense around the center of power. Kōriyama castle, moreover, lay only twenty miles removed from the former site of the Ishiyama Hongan monastery, where he had begun on the construction of his new headquarters of Osaka castle, and he often stayed at his stepbrother's new headquarters.

It was during this period, while his power was at its apex, that Hideyoshi planned to make the next great moves in his military campaign to pacify the country and complete Nobunaga's work. Retiring from his position as *kanpaku* and assuming the title of *taikō* (retired regent) he turned all his energies to the submission of Shikoku and Kyushu, and the subjugation of the powerful Hōjō at Odawara castle. Huge sums of money were required to finance these massive campaigns, and in a feudal age the chief source of revenue was the tax levied upon a plot of land's rice yield.

163

*Toyotomi Hidenaga,
who confiscated the
Yagyū domains*

To determine the tax that could be levied, it was of crucial importance to know the exact dimensions of the lands under their own rule and that of their vassals. And here lay the great problem. The anarchy of the preceding century had thoroughly upset the pattern of land rights that had been in place during the early Muromachi period. As the fighting had spread, so had the often conflicting claims by local military rulers over ever more fragmented pieces of land, until even they themselves were often in the dark as to size and yield of the domains under their control. Nobunaga had already made an attempt to bring some order into this chaos by conducting vast surveys, or *kenchi*, throughout the provinces under his control, shedding light on crucial information such as area, yield, ownership, and tenancy. Though large in total area, those provinces had still been limited in number, and thus, as he was nearing the completion of his predecessor's goal, Hideyoshi set about to conduct nationwide land survey. Not surprisingly, the *taikō kenchi*, as it came to be known, was most rigorously executed in the provinces under his immediate control, such as Yamato, under the governorship of his stepbrother Hidenaga.

It was somewhere in the fall of 1585 that Toyotomi Hidenaga's land surveyors set out along the Yagyū Michi. Already they had charted large tracts of the province. They had begun in the Nara basin, the most fertile area, where rice yields were highest. Now they had set their sights on the mountainous region of Kasagi, just east of Nara and home to the Yagyū domains. It was not long before they discovered that the Yagyū clan had gone into hiding and that, in the wake of Matsunaga Hisahide's demise, no taxes had been levied over their domains. Their actions were as drastic as the letter of Hideyoshi's policies prescribed. All of the Yagyū domains, covering an area with a total yield of more than two thousand *koku*, were confiscated forthwith.

Now the Yagyū were reduced to true fugitives, with no castle to live in, no land to defend, and no lord to serve. In a

Yagyū Michi, the old road that connects Yagyū with the temple town of Nara

165

world in which everything depended on this inseparable trinity, the future of the Yagyū clan seemed doomed. Never in its long history, a history that had spanned the better part of five centuries, had the fate of the Yagyū clan reached such appalling depths. Even their unsurpassed mastery of the sword, an art that had seen them through so many vicissitudes, now seemed reduced to a useless anachronism, unable to hold its own against an art of warfare in which the *teppō*, the foreign rifle, took pride of place.

For the fifty-eight-year-old Muneyoshi it was too much. As family patriarch he felt responsible for the plight in which they found themselves. There seemed no end to the dreadful succession of calamities, and when, in the winter of 1587, it was followed by the death of his father, Ieyoshi, he renounced the world and took the tonsure under the name of Sekishūsai or "Stone Vessel." The significance of that name and the depth of Muneyoshi's despair is revealed in a poem from his own hand, the opening lines of which read:

> Without a means to live
> I make the art of swordsmanship
> my refuge, my sad repose.
> It is good for hiding places
> yet in strife it has no use
> For though I may win contests
> I am but a stone vessel
> Unable to cross the sea of life.

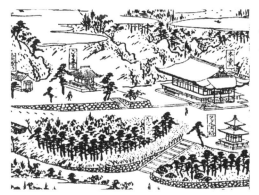

*The Enjō temple
as it was in
Munenori's day*

Ten more years Yagyū Muneyoshi remained in hiding, working a small plot of land belonging to the Enjō temple to feed his family, while drilling his youngest son in the techniques of the Shinkage school of fencing. Only the occasional rumor, gleaned by his wife and daughters from the nervous villagers of Ōhirao gave him and his son cause to emerge from the preoccupations of the day and consider in what way their future might be affected by Toyotomi Hideyoshi's massive campaigns: his subjugation of Shikoku and Kyushu in 1587, his siege of Odawara castle in 1590, and his invasion of Korea in 1592. All these events took place far from the Home Provinces, and while both father and son realized that they were of great importance to the future of the country as a whole, none of them seemed to touch the lives and futures of those who dwelled in the province of Yamato.

It came as a big surprise, then, when, in the late spring of 1594, the tranquillity of Ōhirai was disturbed by a group of mounted warriors. They were retainers of Kuroda Nagamasa,

167

and soon the word spread that they were looking for a certain Yagyū Muneyoshi.

Muneyoshi knew Nagamasa, though not closely. During the middle of the 1580s, when he had traveled the Home Provinces on one of his *musha shugyō*, he had visited the old Kuroda estate in the province of Harima, an estate that had been bestowed on the Kuroda by Hideyoshi in reward for their services in the wake of the Honnō Rebellion. Muneyoshi had been warmly received by Nagamasa, a warrior widely known and respected for his martial prowess, and had given him a demonstration of the *mutōtori*, a technique by which one could disarm an opponent without the use of one's sword. The technique had been invented by none other than Aisu Ikō, the founder of the Kage no Ryū, and had been passed on to Muneyoshi by Kamiizumi Nobutsuna. What Muneyoshi could not understand was why Nagamasa's men would want to visit him now. Indeed, he failed to see why they should be in the Home Provinces at all. It had been more that seven years, after all, since Nagamasa and his clansmen had uprooted and moved to the province of Buzen, on Kyushu, where they had received vast tracts of land in reward for their services during Hideyoshi's campaign to subdue the island. Yet something told the old warrior, who had now reached the respectful age of sixty-six, that Nagamasa's men had not come in anger.

It was with great relief that Muneyoshi found his instincts had not lied. Nagamasa's men explained that they had come from Fushimi, where Hideyoshi had begun on the reconstruction of the local castle. Situated on an elevation

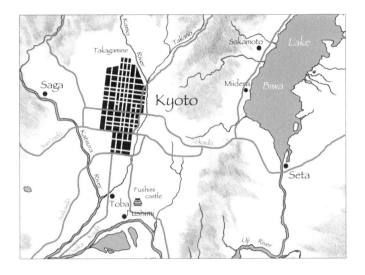

on the northern bank of the Uji River, Fushimi castle had been completed only a few years earlier. It had been intended for Hideyoshi's retirement, after he had conquered Korea and China. That conquest, however, although begun in a blaze of glory, had not gone as planned. After landing in force at Pusan with one hundred and fifty thousand troops, his generals had captured the capital Seoul within little more than a month, and the more northern town of Pyŏngyang within another. Exactly one year later the roles had been reversed. A large Chinese force had driven the Japanese troops back into the peninsula's southernmost provinces, while the superior Korean navy had decimated the invasion fleet. Hideyoshi's generals were in such difficulty that they felt obliged to sue for peace. Lengthy negotiations followed, and at last the Ming court

169

Fushimi castle

agreed to send an embassy to Japan. Hideyoshi had decided that he would receive them at Fushimi castle, conveniently situated close to the capital and the imperial palace. To accommodate such a grand occasion the castle needed drastic expansion, As many as six *zōei bugyō*, or "construction magistrates," were put in charge of the project, while many of the warlords whose forces were not stationed on the Korean Peninsula were ordered to lend assistance and provide the work force of more than twenty thousand men, who were to work on the project day and night.

One of the generals ordered to assist in the reconstruction of Fushimi castle was the eastern warlord Tokugawa Ieyasu. He had set up camp at Takagamine, on the bank of the Kamo River, on the northern outskirts of the capital. Kuroda Nagamasa, who had participated in the Korean campaign with some five thousand men, had visited Ieyasu at his temporary abode on his return to Japan. The warlords knew each other well. They shared a love of military matters and the conversation had soon turned to the Korean campaign, the mainland warriors, and their art of fighting.

The Koreans, Nagamasa conceded, were good warriors, but it had only been their overwhelming number, he assured his host, that had enabled them to drive the Japanese troops out of Pyöngyang and Seoul. Eventually the conversation drifted to matters closer to home, and it was with some relief that both warlords concluded that, where it came to the art of fencing, the Japanese warrior had no equal on the continent. Roused by the content of their conversation, Ieyasu had asked Nagamasa wether he knew of any great swordsmen in the surrounding area who might come and entertain them with his skills. The latter had immediately cast his mind back to the time he had lived in Kawachi, when an aging swordsman from the neighboring province of Yamato had impressed him with his superlative fencing skills. He told Ieyasu that he knew of a warrior from the province of Yamato, a certain Yagyū Munenori, who had

Old map of Fushimi castle

visited him on a *musha shugyō*, and who had impressed him with a technique by which he could disarm an opponent without the use of his sword.

Thus it was that, on June 21, 1594, Yagyū Muneyoshi and his son Munenori rode into Ieyasu's camp at Takagamine, dismounted, and made their appearance. In the tradition of the times Ieyasu's quarters were encircled by a high curtain, emblazoned with his family crest and held up by a row of pikes placed at regular intervals. It was a fine day and the warlord was seated outside his tent, on a low chair covered with the hide of a deer. Rising from his seat, Ieyasu took a *bokken* and placed himself at the middle of the enclosure. It was filled with his bannermen, as well as a number of dignitaries, and it was with a degree of self-awareness that the warlord turned toward Muneyoshi and challenged him, daring him to take his weapon without the use of his own. No sooner had he spoken than he charged at Muneyoshi, raising the wooden sword and uttering a *kiai* at the top of his voice as he brought down the weapon on Muneyoshi's head. Yet instead of recoiling, Muneyoshi moved in upon Ieyasu. The moment they were about to clash, he swiftly moved to the left and, swivelling round on the ball of his left heel in unison with his opponent, seized the hilt of the *bokutō* from below with his left hand, causing the warlord to lose his balance and tumble forward. A nervous silence descended on the encampment as Ieyasu rose and calmly brushed the dirt from his tunic. Any lesser man might have felt humiliated, insulted, but not Ieyasu. He, instead, praised the aging swordsman, who was his senior by fourteen years. He

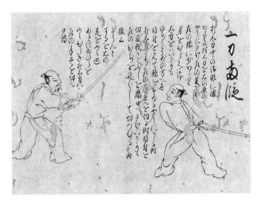

Yagyū technique

offered him to join his retinue of *shihan*, his personal fencing instructors, and expressed his eagerness to learn more about the Shinkage school of fencing. Muneyoshi readily accepted. And, while the portent of the offer was still sinking in, Ieyasu called his scribe and made him draft a written pledge in which he solemnly vowed not to "divulge to anyone that what I have learned, be they my parents or children, before I have received my *inka*."

It was a remarkable reversal of fortune that the gods had granted the aging Yamato swordsman. For two long decades he and his family had lived in obscurity, not knowing what setbacks the dawning of each new day would bring. Now he had become a personal fencing instructor with a stipend of two hundred *koku* to one of the most powerful warlords in the Japanese realm—a warlord whom even the great *taikō* Toyotomi Hideyoshi had deemed it prudent to keep an ally.

Over the next few years Muneyoshi faithfully served Ieyasu in the capacity of *shihan*. In this, Muneyoshi was not alone. Befitting a warlord of his position, Ieyasu's retinue included a host of other swordsmen from different schools of fencing. Chief among them at this point in time was Ono Tadaaki, the propagator of Itō Ittōsai's Ittō-ryō. There were other swordsmen, of equally reputable schools of swordsmanship. One of them, Okuyama Kyūgasai Kimishige, was, like Muneyoshi, a one-time disciple of Kamiizumi Nobutsuna, and had gone on to found his own particular strand called the Okuyama Shinkage-ryū. Then there was Arima Ōi no Kami Mitsumori, a practitioner of Iizasa Chōisai's Shintō-ryū, whose relative Arima Kihei had dueled with the legendary Miyamoto Musashi. All of them were great swordsmen in their own right, but none of them were from the Home Provinces, nor had any of them been the master of his own castle as Muneyoshi had once been. That, however, was more than twenty years ago, and now the old warrior had to

Arima Kihei, who had dueled with the legendary Miyamoto Musashi

adjust to the life of a retainer. Instead of giving orders, he had to follow orders, and in order to hold on to his position he had to compete with equally talented swordsmen, many of whom were far less advanced in years.

Muneyoshi's newly won position had its advantages too. No longer need he worry about the protection of his domains, and his stipend of two hundred *koku* was more than enough to support him and his family. Being part of Ieyasu's retinue also allowed him to witness from close quarters the great events that occurred on the center stage of national politics in the closing years of the sixteenth century. He was at Fushimi with Ieyasu when a great earthquake in the Kyoto basin almost completely destroyed the castle, undoing within a few minutes much of the work that had been done over the previous years. That was in 1596, in the first year of Keichō. Hideyoshi had ordered his *zōei bugyō* to immediately resume work, but the castle was not ready in time, and when the Chinese embassy reached the capital in the last month of the same year, he was forced to invite them to Osaka castle instead.

The swordsman had also witnessed less auspicious events—events, ironically, that had been set in motion by happy tidings. In 1593 Hideyoshi's mistress Yodogimi bore him a second son, whom he named Hideyori. To the *taikō* Hideyori's arrival was an immense relief. His first son, Tsurumatsu, had died in infancy two years before. That premature death and his own advancement in age had led him to appoint his nephew Hidetsugu (a Mitsuyoshi by descent) as his rightful heir. Bestowing on him the title of *kanpaku*, he

Toyotomi Hidetsugu, target of Hideyoshi's wrath

installed Hidetsugu in the Jurakudai, the official residence of men appointed to this high post. The new *kanpaku* took his task seriously and it was not long before his policies began to clash with those of his adoptive father. The latter had initially accepted these frictions as part of the process of succession, but with the birth of his natural son they became an irritant. His growing dislike of Hidetsugu was fanned by his almost obsessive love for his natural son, and within a year of Hideyori's birth, he began to conspire against his appointed heir. Rumors began to make their way around the capital, rumors that the *kanpaku* was leading a dissolute life, that he enjoyed killing, that he was given to liquor and lechery, and, most outrageously, that he was plotting to capture Osaka castle by corrupting its guards. In a world in which all news was communicated by word of mouth, the rumors soon became fact, and before long the dutiful Hidetsugu, whose chief pastime was the collection of old writings, was publicly branded as the *sasshō kanpaku*, the "murderous regent."

Hideyoshi's punishment was as swift as it was brutal. In the summer of 1595 he banished Hidetsugu to the Kōyasan monastery among the Kii Mountains in the northern part of the province of Kii. Shortly afterward he sent his adoptive son a messenger with an order to commit ritual suicide. Hidetsugu's removal, however, was not enough. Jealous of everything that might threaten the succession of his natural son, Hideyori, the despot proceeded to persecute with a vengeance all the members of Hidetsugu's household, from his three infant children to his concubines and the many other women in his service. All were dragged through the long and dusty streets of the capital, right up to the execution grounds at Sanjōgawara, the river bed of the Kamo River at the height of the capital's third main road, where travelers from the Tōkaidō entered the city. There, in front of a gibbet adorned with Hidetsugu's head, they were stabbed to death one by one until the ground was sodden with their spilled blood. Following this act of barbarity

The Kōyasan monastery, scene of a tragic death

Hideyoshi ordered that all physical reminders of his adoptive son be destroyed. The order was carried out to the last letter and over the following weeks all the buildings in which the hapless *kanpaku* had dwelled, including the Jurakudai, were torn down, never to rise again.

Muneyoshi witnessed these gruesome events from close quarters and was present when, shortly after, Ieyasu and the other great warlords were called to a council at Osaka castle where all were made to sign a written oath in which they solemnly pledged their allegiance to the Hideyori.

Three years later, in the summer of 1598, feeling his strength ebbing and realizing his end was drawing near, Hideyoshi called into life the institutions that would ensure Hideyori's succession. Drawing on the organs of state of the Muromachi Bakufu that had survived Nobunaga's period of rule, he formed two councils of five men each. The board with most authority was the *go-tairō*, the Council of (five) Regents. Its members were Tokugawa Ieyasu, Maeda Toshiie, Mōri Terumoto, Uesugi Kagekatsu, and Ukita Hideie. These men, his most trusted vassals, were to safeguard continued Toyotomi rule. The second organ of state was that of the *go-bugyō*, the Council of (five) Commissioners. Its members were Ishida Mitsunari, Asano Nagamasa, Maeda Geni, Mashita Nagamori, and Natsuka Masaie. The *bugyō* were directly responsible to the *tairō* and in charge of the administrative and day-to-day affairs of government. Satisfied that he had done all he could to secure his son's succession, on September 5, Hideyoshi once again called Ieyasu to his bedside and made him swear once more that he

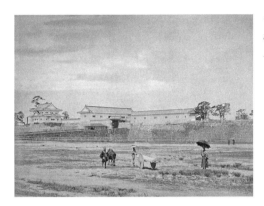

Osaka castle at the end of the 19th century

would obey his every injunction. Two weeks later the *taikō* was dead and the future of his heir in the hands of Ieyasu and the other *go-tairō*.

Ieyasu had dutifully complied with all of Hideyoshi's wishes, as had all the other warlords—to do otherwise was to court certain disaster. Hideyoshi did not question Ieyasu's loyalty and had made him his guardian, with instructions to see to Hideyori's appointment as *kanpaku* when the time was ripe. Ieyasu on his part was, at least for the time being, content with the arrangement. The death one year later of Maeda Toshiie, the new lord of Osaka castle, made him the most powerful warlord among the five *tairō*, a position that he underscored with characteristic decisiveness when, on Toshiie's death, he moved into the western wing of the vacated castle and was recognized by the other *tairō* as the *tenka dono*, the undisputed "lord of the realm."

Yagyū Muneyoshi was now seventy years old and had been in Ieyasu's service for four years. For his family it had been a period of remarkable recovery, but not without its setbacks.

One year before his death, in one of his increasingly frequent yet always unpredictable fits of anger, Hideyoshi broke the fragile truce that had been established with China and sent another large invading force to the Korean Peninsula. Among the one hundred thousand warriors that had been ferried across the Tsushima Straits was one of Muneyoshi's grandsons, Yoshikatsu's oldest son, Kyūsaburō. Yet in sharp relief with the mood of invincibility that accompanied the first invasion, this mission was dominated by a feeling of doom. This mood had already taken hold of the warriors during the passage, which was fraught with so many difficulties that close to half a year passed before all the troops had been landed at Pusan. The defeatist spirit persisted on land, deepening as winter set in. Instead of thrusting northward, toward the capital of Seoul, the invasion force began to ensconce itself in the castles it began to build at Ulsan, Chinju, and Sunch'on, all situated along the southern coast, where they could be supplied with victuals and other provisions over water. These were not makeshift fortifications, but huge strongholds, built to the exacting standards of Japanese craftsmanship, with massive stone walls and deep moats, the construction of which was labor-intensive and time consuming. Three of the expedition's chief generals now took it upon themselves to see to the construction and defense of the three strongholds: Katō Kiyomasa at Ulsan, Shimazu Yoshihiro at Chinju, and

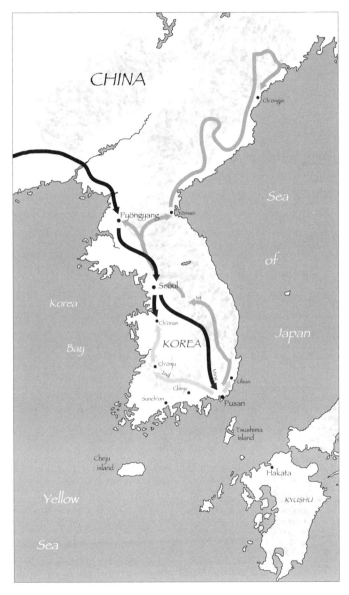

Konishi Yukinaga at Sunch'on. Informed by their spies that the strongholds were not yet completed, the Koreans and Chinese commanders launched a massive counter offensive. Toward the end of 1597, they departed from Seoul at the head of some seventy thousand troops. Proceeding rapidly southward along the peninsula's three main roads, they reached the city of Ulsan within a few days, taking the busily preoccupied Japanese utterly by surprise.

Muneyoshi's grandson had been attached to the regiment of Katō Kiyomasa, the general in charge of Ulsan's defense. The general had been away that day, visiting the nearby port to expedite the slow supply of victuals, which were urgently needed in the cold continental winter. Hearing of the attack he immediately rushed back, and it was only in the chaos of a town under siege and the cover of night that he was able to steal back into the Japanese stronghold. By the next evening the Koreans and Chinese had recaptured the city's outskirts and killed a thousand Japanese warriors. Over the next few

Katō Kiyomasa, the general under whom Muneyoshi's grandson served during the second Korean campaign

days casualties rose on both sides, well into the thousands. Fighting was soon concentrated around the periphery of the building site, where the Japanese sought to use to their advantage those sections of the castle that were close to completion, while the attackers sought to make the most of those that were not.

After a month of siege warfare the position of the Japanese was dire. Reports were coming in at the headquarters of the Ming army that within the castle the Japanese were by now:

> reduced to the eating of paper and leather, anything to fill their groaning stomachs, while they seek to quench their thirst by drinking their own urine, and when they prepare the food they have, they give it to their riflemen first, leaving the others to perish from starvation.

One of the countless warriors to come to this wretched end was Yagyū Kyūsaburō. It was from none other than Kuroda Nagamasa, the man who had rescued the Yagyū family from the brink of ruin that the old Muneyoshi received the news of his grandson's tragic end. Kuroda had been part of a relief party of some ten thousand troops assembled to lift the siege. In this they miraculously succeeded, but not without first suffering heavy casualties themselves. When they did finally force their way through to the castle, they came upon a scene from hell. The inner court was strewn with the remains of dead warriors, Japanese, Chinese, and Korean alike, fallen where they had fought, and frozen in grotesque embraces by the indiscriminate cold of winter.

The siege of Ulsan castle, in which Kyūsaburō lost his life

The incomplete and blood-streaked walls resounded with the wail of the dying, while the air was thick with the stench of putrefied flesh. Among the countless corpses that Nagamasa and his men inspected that day was that of thirty-year-old Kyūsaburō, still clutching the hilt of his rusted sword. It was of some consolation to the old Muneyoshi that his grandson had died in the line of duty. At the same time Kyūsaburō's life, like the lives of so many other young and promising men in these years of turmoil seemed to have been lost in vain, cut short as it was only fifty miles from where the young warrior and his comrades had landed almost a year before. His sentiments must have been shared by the Japanese generals in charge of the invasion force. After several more months of senseless slaughter, the news of Hideyoshi's death finally opened the way to a renewed settlement with their Korean and Chinese counterparts. Hideyoshi's grand plan for the conquest of Korea and China had run its course—the dream was over.

184

Muneyoshi's grief over the loss of his grandson was tempered by the knowledge that at least the future of his remaining offspring was secure. Two of his sons were by now monks. As such they posed no financial burden, except of course for the seasonal contributions his clan was expected to make to their temple's upkeep.

His fourth son, Muneaki, too, had seen action on the mainland. Muneaki had entered the service of Kobayakawa Hideaki, a warlord from Kyushu, who controlled much of western part of the island. It had been only a year since that the sixteen-year-old Hideaki had become master of Najima castle, just north of Hakata, after his adoptive father, Takakage, suddenly passed away. The latter had built the castle a decade earlier, when it served as Hideyoshi's first foothold during his campaign to subdue the island once and for all. It had been in return for Takakage's services that Hideyoshi had given him control over the provinces of Chikuzen, Chikugo, as well as parts of Hizen. Takakage and

Today only the main gate of Najima castle remains

his ten thousand warriors had also fought hard during the Korean campaign, when they crushed the great Ming army just north of Seoul, forcing it to retreat all the way to Pyöngyang. Yagyū Muneaki had fought on the continent under the command of the young Hideaki, but instead of a repeat of his father's successes, the latter's youthful rashness resulted in a number of failures. Shortly before his death Hideyoshi had ordered him to leave his domains in Kyushu and remove himself to a small fiefdom in the northern regions of Echizen. By the time the order reached Najima castle the *taikō* had already passed away, and through the mediation of Ieyasu the young warlord was allowed to hold on to his possessions. Muneaki, too, had remained in Kyushu, continuing to serve his young lord.

Only his fifth son, Munenori, in spite of his many qualities, his great talent at swordsmanship, had not yet found a niche for himself. It was the source of some anxiety to the old swordsman that his youngest son had not yet found the means to realize his ambitions and live up to the great expectations he had raised in his father.

While troubled by these thoughts, Muneyoshi was also beginning to feel the weight of old age. The demands of Ieyasu's busy life were exceedingly high, especially in the wake of Hideyoshi's death, when the eastern warlord was moving to strengthen his position among the other nine members on the two councils. Contrary to Hideyoshi's intentions there was little unity among the *tairō* and *bugyō*. Soon after his death the two councils began to fall apart into two rival factions, one coalescing around Ieyasu, the other around the western warlord Ishida Mitsunari. The real power the factions exercised was not expressed in the official position their members occupied, but in the extent of the territories that they and their adherents controlled, as this was the basis for the military muscle each faction could bring to the fore. To extend the power of his faction and consolidate his position Ieyasu began to fall back on the age-old and trusted method of intermarriage, binding to him and his adherents those warlords who could tip the balance of power in their favor. This led him to travel the length and breadth of the country, and for the aging Muneyoshi, who was often called upon to provide escort for his master's many guests, as well as demonstrate his skills for their amusement, the burden of office became heavier with every day. Aware that he had reached a point in his life where he could no longer fulfill his obligations, he approached his lord with the request to be dismissed and that his place be taken by his youngest son, Munenori. To his immense relief Ieyasu acceded to both, thanking him for the services he had rendered and gratefully accepted the swordman's plea to be replaced by his son. He predicted that great events were afoot. They were not far in the offing, and he assured the old man that Munenori would play his role in their unfolding.

Munenori had been in the service of the *tenka dono* for little more than a year when the prescience of Ieyasu's words to his father was revealed. Ever since Hideyoshi's death Ieyasu had watched with Argus eyes how Mitsunari had furtively

Aizu Wakamatsu castle, headquarters of Uesugi Kagekatsu

positioned himself for a major confrontation, forging secret alliances with other western warlords without giving his opponents any direct cause to accuse him of treachery. What Ieyasu needed was a ploy, an excuse by which to draw the shrewd and wily Mitsunari from his den and expose his treachery to the other *go-tairō*.

That opportunity presented itself in the spring of 1600, when reports began to reach Osaka castle from Ieyasu's informants in the Kantō that none other than one of his fellow *go-tairō*, the northern warlord Uesugi Kagekatsu, was reinforcing his positions in the province of Aizu. He had issued secret orders to his vassals to prepare their strongholds for war and had even begun on the construction of a new castle at the center of the Aizu Basin. Like Kenshin, Kagekatsu had always been a nuisance, but with his power base far removed from the center of power and only half the talent of his adoptive father, he never posed a serious threat to Ieyasu's designs. Indeed, he now provided Ieyasu with the perfect pretext to act. Already Ieyasu had repeatedly summoned Kagekatsu to come down to Osaka castle and explain his conduct. As Ieyasu had anticipated, the belligerent warlord blatantly ignored the summons and continued to build up his forces around his headquarters of Aizu Wakamatsu castle. The time had come to act, and early in July, Munenori and his fellow *shihan* were instructed to prepare for a long journey; their lord had decided to travel up to Edo castle, and from there to Oyama castle in Shimotsuke, from where he intended to conduct the campaign against the rebellious warlord and, more importantly, await the first signs of Mitsunari's revolt. First, however, he intended to call at Fushimi castle, for it was there that he expected Mitsunari and his fellow conspirators to strike first.

Things that summer went very much as Ieyasu expected. When he arrived in Oyama, on September 1, messengers from his allies in the west of Japan informed him that Ishida Mitsunari had departed from his stronghold of Sawayama castle in Ōmi and, on August 27, laid siege to Fushimi castle with some forty thousand troops. Among the warlords who had chosen Mitsunari's side were Mōri Hidemoto, Ukita Hideie, and Kobayakawa Hideaki, all men from the west of Japan. They and their fathers had been forced to bend to the will of Ieyasu's predecessors, but they had done so reluctantly and had resented the influence the Kantō warlords had come to exert, first over Kyoto, then over the Home Provinces, and finally even over Japan's western provinces. Ieyasu, in turn, had always been wary of them, their general reluctance to recognize his authority, and their attempts to thwart him at every turn. Now the time had come to over-come their opposition once and for all and settle matters in his favor and in favor of a truly unified country.

On his departure from Fushimi castle he had left Torii Mototada and some fifteen hundred of his best warriors in charge of the castle's defense. Both men knew that it was far too small a force to withstand a sustained assault, but it was enough to keep them tied down long enough for Ieyasu to take care of Kagekatsu. He had never intended to pit his men against those of the rebellious warlord and be pinned down in the north with his rear vulnerable to attack. Yet he knew that it was that very assumption that had led Mitsunari to show his colors and move against Fushimi castle. It was all he required. Now he could rightfully claim that Mitusnari and his allies were rebels who needed to be dealt with.

On September 2 he ordered all the vassal warlords who had joined him on his northern expedition to assemble at Oyama, where he convened a council in which he set out the

The scene of the Oyama war council

strategy by which he intended to counter Mitsunari's challenge. A number of warlords were to return home to their domains in order to raise yet more troops. Most of the gathered warlords, however, would lead their troops down the Tōkaidō to Kiyosu castle, just west of Nagoya. There they were to await the arrival of the others, as well as Ieyasu's son, Hidetada, who would lead the rest of Ieyasu's troops down the Nakasendō.

On September 6 Ieyasu called to his side a number of his closest retainers, among them Yagyū Munenori. This, he told them, was the moment for which he had been waiting. During the four days that had passed since the council he had written a large number of letters. They were addressed to allied warlords throughout the country and it was the task of Munenori and the others to ensure that they were delivered to the addressees without fail. Ieyasu urged the assembled men to go about their duty with great care, but also with alacrity, for there was no time to lose if they were to intercept Mitsunari and his allies before they had passed beyond the province of Mino. To Munenori's utter surprise one of the letters was addressed to none other than his father, who had again retired to his native village of Yagyū, where he had entered a small temple and taken the tonsure.

Deeply aware of the importance of his mission Munenori traveled without rest. Only the endurance of his horse forced him to make the occasional stop at one of the Tōkaidō's many post stations for food and water. Taking the shortest route possible Munenori covered the huge distance in only five days. It was a three-hundred-mile journey and while most of the domains through which he passed were under the control of Ieyasu and his allies, one could never be sure where danger lurked, especially in Mino, where the western warlords could count on the support of Nobunaga's descendants at Gifu castle. His journey, however, passed without incident, and it was with immense relief, and utterly exhausted that, late in the afternoon of September 11, he drew up his horse outside his father's modest abode in Yagyū village. The last thing he saw before he was finally overcome by sleep was his father holding up to the light the unfolded piece of paper and absorbing its content with an air of grave solemnity.

In his letter to Muneyoshi, Ieyasu urged the his former *shihan* to seek out all *rōnin* in his area and make contact with Tsutsui Sadatsugu, the successor to Tsutsui Junkei, the former ruler of Yamato who had been forced by Hideyoshi to move his seat of power to Ueno in the neighboring province of Iga. Munenori was quick to inform him that Sadatsugu had been among the many warlords who had joined Ieyasu on his campaign against Uesugi Kagekatsu. He related how, on the eve of his departure from Oyama, all the gathered warlords had attended a council convened by Ieyasu. Sadatsugu, however, had not been among them. Why he did not know. All he knew was that within only a few days of his arrival at Oyama, Sadatsugu and his large contingent of warriors had hurriedly departed. All these activities, of course, had been shrouded in a veil of secrecy, and he knew neither what had been discussed at the meeting, nor the reason for Sadatsugu's sudden departure.

Having lived in close proximity to Ieyasu for several years, Muneyoshi had no difficulty in following the warlord's line of thought. The news of the fall of Fushimi castle had already reached him, and he knew that this was the moment that Ieyasu had been waiting for. The combined force of all the chieftains who had marched up to Aizu and attended the council would certainly run into the tens of thousands. It was only with their help that Ieyasu could hope to subdue Mitsunari and his allies, whose combined strength must also run into the tens of thousands. Tsutsui Sadatsugu, too, was a powerful warlord, who could muster at least several thousand well-trained warriors. Muneyoshi had stayed in close contact with his relatives among the Nakanobō, and on his various *musha shugyō*, he had frequently visited them at their new abode on Sadatsugu's estate in Ueno. He had witnessed from close quarters how their lord had made the most of his

Tsutsui Sadatsugu, constable of Iga province

193

forced removal. He had put a lot of effort in the recruitment and training of troops, and in 1587, he had begun the construction of Ueno castle, a huge stronghold, right at the center of his new domains.

The old man also knew that the recently erected castle had been the very reason for Sadatsugu's hasty return. On his departure, Sadatsugu had left the castle in the care of his brother. But during his absence western forces under the command of Shinjō Naoyori had marched into Iga. The Shinjū clan hailed from Ōmi, where they had long served the Asai, who been sworn enemies of Ieyasu ever since he and Nobunaga had crushed them and the Asakura at Ane River in 1570. During the eighties Naoyori had become a trusted retainer of Hideyoshi, for whom he reduced a number of castles throughout the Home Provinces. Now he was the master of Takatsuki castle in Settsu. Given his bond of loyalty toward the Asai, as well as the geographic position of his domains he had joined the western forces. Upon Mitsunari's

Ueno castle, headquarters of Tsutsui Sadatsugu

revolt he had seized his chance to expand westward into
Yamato and Iga and marched on the strategic stronghold of
Ueno castle. Sadatsugu had left behind only a skeleton force
and his young and inexperienced brother had fled east across
the mountains to the protection of the Kōyasan monastery.
It had not been long after these events had taken place that
Sadatsugu had returned in full force and recaptured the castle without much trouble. All, then, was set for the Yagyū
clan to play its own modest but valuable role in Ieyasu's great
scheme to unify the country. That same evening they sent
out word across the region, urging all befriended clans to
join them the next day, when they would cross the border
into Iga and put themselves under the command of Tsutsui
Sadatsugu, the lord of Ueno castle.

It was September 12 when Ieyasu crossed the bridge over the
wide moat of Edo castle and entered the imposing gate to
his eastern headquarters. Following the council of warlords
at Oyama he had ordered his Kantō allies to keep Kagekatsu
in check and returned to Edo castle, where he intended to
ready himself for the final confrontation with Ishida
Mitsunari and his allies.

Events were now unfolding in rapid succession. On his
arrival, he learned that four days earlier Fushimi castle had
fallen after ten days of intense fighting in which Torii
Mototada and all his men had given their lives. A week later
he learned that, having captured Fushimi castle, Mitsunari
and his allies had proceeded eastward along the Tōkaidō,

Bridge of Edo castle

entering the province of Mino, where, on September 17, they entered the small stronghold of Ōgaki castle without encountering any resistance. It appeared they wanted to entrench themselves in Mino, where they could count on the support of Oda Hidenobu.

The *tenka dono* was not in the least perturbed by these tidings. He had given the two great armies that departed on the day following the council enough time to reach their destinations—something that was confirmed by the news, shortly after his arrival, that the force that had marched down the Tōkaidō had reached the stronghold of Kiyosu according to plan. Ieyasu himself, however, did not move from Edo castle. First he wanted to ascertain the loyalty of his commanders in the field, and that loyalty could only be expressed in military feats. Such was the purport of a message delivered to the gathered forces at Kiyosu on September 26, and it had the desired effect. Two days later a contingent of five thousand men under the command of

Ikeda Terumasa crossed the Kiso River upstream to attack Gifu castle in force. They came under dense rifle fire from Oda Hidenobu's troops across the river, forcing them at first to retreat. Then, however, the scales tipped. A second large eastern contingent, under the command of Fukushima Masanori, had crossed the river farther downstream by means of a fleet of small boats under the cover of night. At first the Oda forces offered fierce resistance, but when they were threatened with being cut off, Hidenobu ordered his men to retreat to the castle.

At early daybreak on September 30 the Ikeda and Fukushima forces launched a massive attack on Gifu castle. Within hours Masanori's men had forced one of the castle's gates and made their way into the castle's second compound, the last line of defense protecting the keep where Oda

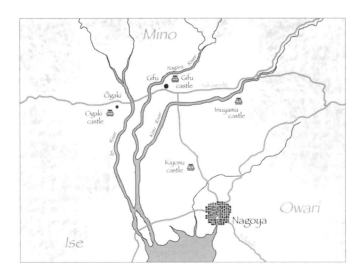

Gifu castle and its castle town in Munenori's day

Hidenobu and his family were holding out. Not much later Terumasa's men forced their way into the last compound, setting sections of it afire and hurling their banner into the castle's keep shouting "today, we are the first to breach the enemy's castle." High up in the keep, Hidenobu, realizing the game was up, prepared to commit ritual suicide. But he was prevailed upon by his retainers to surrender and go into seclusion in Gifu's Entoku temple.

Hearing that Gifu castle had fallen, the master of nearby Inuyama castle also surrendered. All the commanders who had led their troops along the Tōkaidō now ordered their men to advance westward, toward Ōgaki castle.

Mitsunari was stunned by the swiftness with which his enemies had turned the scales on him. In his plans the castles of Ōgaki, Gifu, and Inuyama had featured as a barrier to guard the gateway to the capital and the western provinces. It had also seemed the perfect base from which to launch his intended strike against Ieyasu's home province of Mikawa and the Kantō beyond. Now those plans were rendered futile. Within only a few days the eastern army had captured two of his Mino strongholds, and now threatened to do the same with the castle where he and his allies had gathered. He panicked and ordered his troops to press forward, toward Gifu, and to throw up a line of defense along the eastern shores of the Nagara River. However, the strategy backfired, and instead of throwing back the advancing eastern troops, Mitsunari was forced to withdraw to Ōgaki castle at the cost of many a casualty.

Seeing the huge force arrayed against him, Mitsunari now frantically began to write letters to befriended warlords, luring them with the promise of more territories and higher status. His efforts seemed to bear fruit, for over the next few weeks one warlord after the other led their troops into Mino and set up camp in the vicinity of Ōgaki castle. Among them were powerful men such as Ōtani Yoshitsugu, Ukita Hideie, Mōri Hidemoto, Kikkawa Hiroie, and Natsuka Masaie.

Ōgaki castle

199

Their combined forces comprised some thirty thousand men, bringing the total of the western forces close to eighty thousand, roughly twice the number of those arrayed against them. Even warlords of doubtful allegiance made their appearance, among them Kobayakawa Hideaki, who arrived with some eight thousand men in tow.

The eastern army had meanwhile pitched camp at the post station of Akasaka, some three miles northwest of Ōgaki. There were some twenty contingents in all, varying in number from a few hundred to several thousands. The largest was that of Kuroda Nagamasa, who had put well over five thousand warriors in the field. Another large contingent was that of Tsutsui Sadatsugu. With the help of Yagyū Muneyoshi and many of the other local chieftains, Sadatsugu had managed to raise close to three thousand troops. They had departed from Ueno castle toward the end of September and joined their allies shortly after the fall of Gifu and Inuyama castles. There was no sign yet, however, of Ieyasu,

Akasaka, where the eastern army pitched camp

nor of his son Hidetada, who was to lead the second great force along the Nakasendō. And thus they impatiently awaited the arrival of Ieyasu, the great eastern commander who was to conduct the battle against Mitsunari and his western allies, and thereby decide the fate of the nation.

Until the afternoon of October 20 the huge host of warriors, horses, carriers, and camp followers were kept waiting for the *tenka dono* to arrive. That arrival could not have gone unnoticed, neither to them nor to the nearby enemy, for with him he had brought a contingent of thirty thousand troops, bringing the total number of men fighting on his side close to eighty thousand, almost the equivalent of those assembled under Ishida Mitsunari. His arrival was affirmed, when his retainers erected the banners with the Tokugawa crest.

It was not the weather to lift the spirits when Ieyasu dismounted his horse and strode up to his tent to receive the first reports from his commanders in the field. It was fall, the time of year when fierce hurricanes swept in from the southern Pacific to hit the Japanese islands with their relentless force. It seemed that this was exactly what lay in store for the gathered warriors, for the wind was picking up and already a thick veil of rain hung over the landscape, subduing the vivid colors of their armor, the silk banners, and the bright sparkle of the long lances. The air of gloom among the eastern warriors, however, was lifted as if by magic when Ieyasu's messengers reported that all of the enemy forces were still stationed near Ōgaki castle, leaving unprotected the two-mile-wide strip of land that ran westward toward the old barrier town of Sekigahara.

The news seemed too good to be true. Sekigahara's geographic position was just too important to leave unguarded. From here the massive Ibuki Mountains ranged northward, all the way north to Tsuruga, where they plummeted into Tsuruga Bay. Southward from Sekigahara ran the Yōrō Mountains, an equally long and impenetrable stretch of mountains, right into the heart of the mountainous Ise Peninsula. Situated at the point where both mountain ranges met, Sekigahara was considered the gateway between eastern and western Japan. Indeed, its very name, "Plains of the barrier," hailed back to the old Fuwa barrier. That barrier had been erected at the end of the seventh century when, in the wake of the Jinshin Rebellion, Emperor Tenmu had

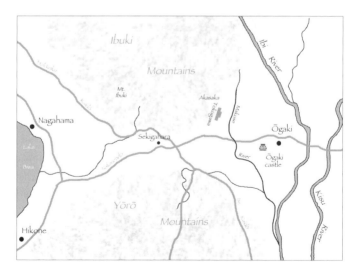

ordered the erection of barriers along the Hokurikudō, the Tōkaidō, and the Nakasendō, the three main roads that connected the capital to the rest of the country. Though the Fuwa barrier itself did not last, throughout Japanese history the passage it had guarded had proven the place of the greatest strategic significance of the three. It had been along here that, following the Heiji Rebellion, Minamoto Yoshitomo and his sons had sought to escape the wrath of Taira Kiyomori by scaling the southern slopes of Mount Ibuki in the midst of winter. And it had been here, too, that Oda Nobunaga, having first subdued Gifu castle, had defeated the Miyoshi and Kitabatake forces, opening up the way to the capital and the Home Provinces.

How could it be that Mitsunari had not seized his advantage? Was it that, as a descendant of western warlords, who had always had unhampered access to the Home Provinces, he did not appreciate the barrier's historic importance? Or was it something else? Was it perhaps the weather? It certainly appeared that the unrelenting rain had gotten to Mitsunari's troops, for Ieyasu's scouts had detected no exceptional movements among them, even after his arrival that afternoon. Only a small group of mounted warriors had loomed up out of the haze to harass his troops stationed along the Makuse River. It was no more than a provocation, and the dreary day drew to a miserable close without any further engagements.

That same evening Ieyasu convened a council of all his commanders in the field. The next day, he told them, they would press eastward, and try to pass the barrier. They would leave behind some five thousand men, far too few to defeat the enemy, but enough to keep them preoccupied for the remainder to pass the barrier into Ōmi province. From there they would march on the castles of Sawayama, Fushimi, and Osaka, the centers of western opposition. It was a bold plan, but if they succeeded the realm would be theirs.

It was in more than one sense that, early in the morning of October 21, Ieyasu felt that he had been rudely roused from his slumber. Two messengers, one from Fukushima Masanori and one from Nishio Mitsunori, had come with disturbing news. It seemed that during the previous evening, while he and his generals had been mapping out their strategy for the next day, a huge contingent of Mitsunari's army had broken camp and begun to march eastward, straight to the plains of Sekigahara. Caught in a blinding rainstorm they had temporarily lost their way, but shortly after midnight they had reached the foot of Mount Sasao, where they had taken up positions on high ground.

For a moment it seemed that Ieyasu had been masterfully outwitted. The mounted warriors who had come down from Ōgaki to harass his soldiers the previous day had been sent with a purpose: to distract the attention of his scouts from the larger troop movements farther afield. He had underestimated Mitsunari. The latter now clearly held the advantage: he had taken the initiative, he now occupied high ground, and it seemed that his forces held the majority, albeit by a narrow margin. Of all these setbacks it was the last one that irked Ieyasu the most. It should have been the other way round. Close to forty thousand more troops had taken the inland route along the Nakasendō under the command of his son, Hidetada. Given that Hidetada had departed from Utsunomiya on the first of October—a week before he himself had departed from Edo—those troops should long since have arrived in Mino. Lines of communication along the inland route, however, had been poor, and the last news he had had from his son was that he was tied down in Shinano, where he had laid siege of Ueda castle. This was an unnecessary diversion. Ueda castle lay not along the Nakasendō, but on a side road, into Echigo and the northwestern provinces.

The seasoned commander soon recovered from his musings. Rising from his field bed he immediately began to issue orders. All troops were to immediately depart for Sekigahara and position themselves against the western forces as best they could. He himself would follow with his own force of thirty thousand men. Only Ikeda Terumasa and his men were to remain behind and cover the rear. Not all of Mitsunari's allies might yet have departed from Ōgaki and if they were quick they might be able to cut them off from Mitsunari's advance force. On their way they ran into such dense fog that Ieyasu was forced to halt his troops for fear of losing his way, and to wait until the clouds lifted. It was five o'clock in the morning before Ieyasu set up his field headquarters at the foot of Mount Momokubari and that his twenty contingents took up their positions on the low-lying fields below the enemy positions. By that time the brunt of the western force had positioned themselves on high ground around the Ikedera pond. Only a few of their contingents, among them those of Mōri Hidemoto, Kikkawa Hiroie, and Natsuka Masaie had lagged behind, but they too had taken up positions on high ground, a few miles south to where Ikeda's men were stationed.

Munenori and the other Yamato warriors who had joined Tsutsui Sadatsugu's army were among the first to take up their positions opposite the enemy. They were now right on the front line, just east of the junction between the Nakasendō and the Hokkoku Kaidō. Even as they took up their positions, one by one the other contingents began to arrive, Flanking them were the Tanaka and the Katō, while behind them those of the Ii, the Matsudaira, and the Miyoshi began to take up their positions. All of them were now no more than a mile removed from enemy lines, and it was with a mixture of fear and relish that Munenori and his fellow warriors awaited the break of dawn.

By eight o'clock, the unrelenting rain of the previous night had somewhat lessened. Shrouds of mist still lingered on the low-lying plain, but the troops were so closely dispersed in the narrow valley that many, including those of the enemy, were visible through the haze. It seemed as if the whole valley was alive with movement as close to two hundred thousand warriors readied themselves for the moment of truth. From where he stood, just over the crest of a hillock, Munenori could clearly make out a black banner with a white cross, the colors of the Shimazu clan. Immediately behind them, at the foot of Mount Tenman stood the troops of Konishi Yukinaga, several thousand in

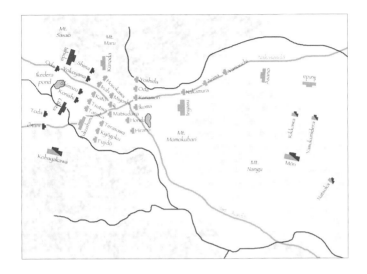

all. And still farther, but more toward the south, an even larger contingent, that of Ukita Hideie, faced Tokugawa's left flank under the command of Fukushima Masanori. Turning his gaze northward, he could make out yet more allied troops, the Hosokawa, the Katō, the Nagaoka. And beyond them, at the foot of Mount Maru, right opposite those of Mitsunari, stood the forces of Kuroda Nagamasa, the man who had played such an important role in the recovery of the Yagyū clan. Now, Munenori realized, was the time to repay Nagamasa and Ieyasu his debt of duty by fighting to the hilt—if need be by laying down his life.

It was more by impulse than by design that, on the morning of October 21, the first shots rang out across the plains of

Fukushima Masanori, eager to take the first enemy head in battle

Sekigahara. Being on the front line, Munenori noticed how, at less than a mile, the troops of Fukushima Masanori were positioned closest to the enemy. This was a position to be envied. Being the first to see action, the commanders at the front line stood the greatest chance of being killed and one of their heads taken. If they survived, however, it would be they who would be the first to take the head of an enemy. That head would immediately be sent back to Ieyasu to inspect and be declared the *ichiban kubi*, the first enemy head to be taken in battle. Needless to say that such a feat would be copiously recompensed after the battle.

Masanori saw his chances go up in smoke when, shortly after eight o'clock, a small group of mounted warriors carrying Matsudaira and Ii banners detached itself from the troops in Munenori's rear and forced their way through the gap between his ranks and those of the Tanaka and Tsutsui. They were led by Ieyasu's fourth son, Matsudaira Tadayoshi, seconded by Ii Naomasa. Their sudden action caused a great degree of consternation among the commanders in the front line, especially among Fukushima Masanori. For no sooner had the contingent rode out into no man's land, they swerved leftward—right in Masanori's line of attack—from where they headed straight for the Ukita and Shimazu banners in the enemy line. Fearing that the two commanders were stealing a march on him, Masanori lost his temper and ordered his riflemen to open fire. The fire was answered by the other side, causing the horsemen to be caught in the crossfire. Within moments of the first exchange of volleys a thin plume of smoke began to climb skyward from the foot of Mount Maru, signaling that, forced by the short temper of his commanders, Kuroda Nagamasa had given orders to commence overall hostilities. The battle of Sekigahara had begun in earnest.

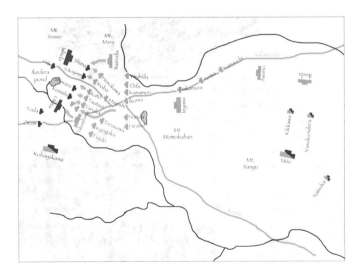

Spotting the signal fires on their right all the commanders along the front line now ordered their musketeers to open fire. Thick plumes of smoke belched forth from the arrayed muzzles to mingle with the heavy morning air, so that within moments the thin stretch of land between the two armies was covered by a dense layer of smog. Then, after several volleys had been exchanged, Munenori could hear the bellowing voice of Tsutsui Sadatsugu, ordering the musketeers to stand aside and let the phalanx of spearmen advance.

As he rushed forward through the acrid smog Munenori could make out little except the flashes of muskets being fired on the other side, shortly followed by a sound not unlike the clattering of hail as the molten lead wreaked havoc among his fellow warriors. By now his senses were being overloaded. Underfoot, the ground reverberated with the rumble of the advancing hordes, while his ears were filled with the battle roar of men and the clatter of their armor. It seemed as if he was swept along on the crest of a wave that

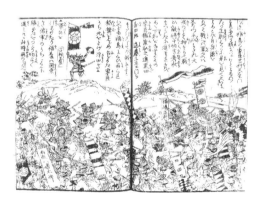

The eastern army opens the attack

Ii Naomasa has wrestled an enemy warrior to the ground

would soon engulf the enemy lines and drown him and his fellow warriors along with it. Within a few agonizing moments they reached the enemy lines. There the mounted Ii and Matsudaira warriors had already picked their men, all, of course, commanders of equal rank. From the corner of his eyes, Munenori spotted how one of them, Ii Naomasa, had wrestled to the ground a western chieftain, and was about to take his head. He did not have the time to see the warrior raise the head aloft, for at that very instant he and his fellow warriors clashed with the Ukita forces, who had dug in the rear end of their *yari* to halt the advance.

Total mayhem now ensued around Munenori as the bulk of the two armies began to clash and warriors began to grapple with each other in man-to-man combat as their ancestors had done for more than five centuries. It was now, in the heat of battle that Munenori, without realizing it, reaped the benefits of his father's patient training over the previous two decades. All the precepts that had been transferred

211

from Aisu Ikō to Kamiizumi Nobutsuna, and from the latter to his father, came now rushing to Munenori's aid as if some invisible hand had beckoned them. He no longer had to think to position his body sideways to his opponent, to make a shield of his fists, to put his weight on his forward knee, and to let the enemy strike first. All these vital techniques now came to him naturally as he stood his ground and tackled one opponent after the other.

Opposition was fierce, especially from the Ukita and Konishi warriors, whose total number was close to twenty thousand. They fought with such determination that by eleven o'clock the eastern forces were pushed back beyond the positions from which they had advanced three hours before. Worried by the way the battle was going, even Ieyasu had become restless, leaving his camp at the foot of Mount Momokubari to take up position at the center of the plain, right behind his forces. Meanwhile the stalemate continued so that even by noon there was no way to tell which way the pendulum would swing.

Mitsunari, too, had begun to lose patience. He sent up smoke signals, urging those commanders who had not yet joined the battle to do so. The most important of these were Mōri Terumoto and Kobayakawa Hideaki. The former, who was still facing the Ikeda contingent from Mount Nangu, now found himself cut off by his vassal Kikkawa Hiroie, who had been persuaded by Ieyasu to change sides in exchange for his lord's domains. Hideaki, who had taken up positions on Mount Matsuo, toward the south of the scene of battle, also failed to move. On the eve of battle, he had arranged with Mitsunari to join the fight on the latter's signal and attack Ieyasu's forces from the rear. Even when Mitsunari sent a messenger over to Mount Matsuo with an urgent request for assistance Hideaki failed to budge.

Ieyasu had also spotted the signal, and he had a good idea why Hideaki was reluctant to fight. While in Edo he had had a letter from Hideaki in which the latter had apologized for the fall of Fushimi castle, professing that circumstances had forced him to participate in the castle's siege. Seeking to capitalize on the Hideaki's sense of guilt, Ieyasu, too had sent missives to Mount Matsuo, but they had come back without any firm commitments. The young warlord was obviously torn by conflicting emotions. What was needed was a good prodding, something to stimulate his senses. Without hesitating Ieyasu ordered his men to open fire on Hideaki's troops, hoping to thereby press him into action and declare himself. Almost immediately Ieyasu's genius for reading men's minds revealed itself. As if roused from a

Kobayakawa Hideaki, ready to charge, but torn by conflicting loyalties

213

slumber, the young warlord stood up in his stirrups, pointed his battle fan in the direction of the Ōtani western forces and called out to his men "aim for the Ōtani ranks."

The effect of Hideaki's defection was almost instantaneous. The eastern warriors, worn down by the repeated setbacks over the previous hours, found new courage as they observed how the six thousand Kobayakawa warriors rushed down the slopes of Mount Matsuo and began to attack the Ōtani and Toda troops, who were wedged between the huge Ukita force and the foot of the mountain. Thus far all of them had bravely withstood the continued assault, but now they began to lose the will to fight, as they found themselves confronted by an army refreshed and superior in numbers. Through superhuman effort they repelled the first attack, driving Hideaki's men back up the mountain's slopes, but

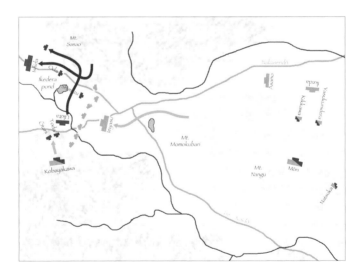

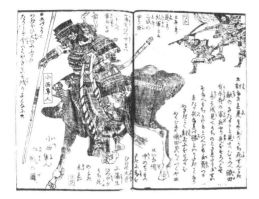

Konishi Yukinaga, being pursued by east- ern warriors

then disaster struck as four other eastern commanders who had taken up positions at the foot of the mountain also changed sides and ordered their men to join those of Hideaki. Under these enormous pressures the ranks of Ōtani and his fellow commanders gradually began to col- lapse until those who were still standing began to retreat northward, into the ranks of the Ukita, and then those of Konishi. Before long they, too, were overwhelmed by the two-pronged assault from the south and the east.

It was with a sinking feeling that Mitsunari watched the remnants of the Ukita and Konishi regiments, the largest he had brought in the field, now run past him, blooded, dishev- elled, disheartened—a sorry sight, if ever there was one. Yet even as the specter of defeat impressed itself on his mind, he realized that it had not been their lack of valor that had lost him his victory, but the failure of the others to come to their rescue. The Mōri, the Natsuka, the Ankokuji, the Shimazu, all of them had stood by idly as their allies were being

215

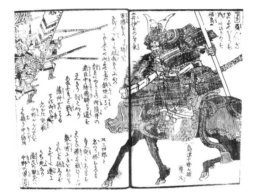

Shimazu Toyohisa, trying to stave off the eastern assault

butchered by the thousands. Unwilling to lose his men in the rescue of others, Shimazu Toyohisa had even ordered his men to erect a *yari fusuma*, a dense wall of *yari*, to keep the fleeing warriors from mingling with his own ranks and thereby weaken them. He was to pay a heavy price for his callous egotism, a price Mitsunari, who had done his bit, was unwilling to pay. One final time he issued a command to his troops, this time to pack up and retreat west along the Hokkoku Kaidō. It was two o'clock. The fighting would go on till late in the afternoon, but Mitsunari's flight confirmed that already the outcome of the battle had been decided.

A strange calm descended over the country in the wake of the Battle of Sekigahara. Things seemed to have gone topsy-turvy as those who had turned on their allies were rewarded and those who had fought valiantly were hunted down to the corners of the realm. Four days after the dust had settled on the plains of the old Seki barrier Takenaka Shigekado, a local chieftain who had joined the eastern forces at the last minute, apprehended Konishi Yukinaga as he was trying to cross the Ibuki Mountains into Ōmi. On November 6 Yukinaga was beheaded at the Rokujōgawara, the embankment of the Kamo River where it intersected with the capital's sixth main road. The blood-stained grounds had been the capital's place of execution since 1156, when the treacherous Taira Kiyomori put to death all the members of his clan who had participated in the Hōgen Rebellion.

Yukinaga's head rolled together with that of a host of others, including that of Ishida Mitsunari, the mastermind behind the western campaign. He had been apprehended by a retainer of Tanaka Yoshimasa, whose troops had faced his at Sekigahara. Following his flight from the scene of battle,

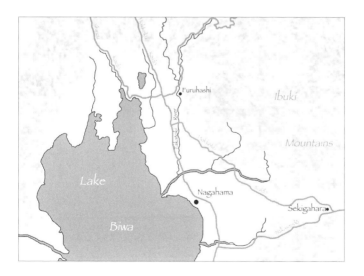

The fugitive Ishida Mitsunari, seized by Tanaka Yoshimasa's retainer

the fugitive had made his way to the village of Furuhashi along the Takatoki River. There he had taken a boat from a local fisherman and, dressing himself in the guise of the boat's owner, rowed upstream to find some form of shelter among the snow clad slopes of the Ibuki Mountains. When he was finally seized, he was found cowering in a cave, suffering from cold, hunger, and a failing health. His fate and that of his allies had been sealed by a widely distributed flyer in which Ieyasu promised high rewards to those who aided in their arrest and punishment by death for all those who abetted in their escape and shelter.

It was, however, with his own son that Ieyasu was most frustrated. Had Hidetada arrived on time the victory at Sekigahara would surely have come at a lower price. Following his departure from Utsunomiya, on October 1, Hidetada had, at first, made good progress. Within a week his force of close to forty thousand men had traversed the Usui pass on the border between Kōzuke and Shinano and reached Komoro castle. At this point his father had just departed from Edo, so that both were well set to simultaneously converge on Gifu, the place of their appointed rendezvous. This was more than feasible. The road through Shinano was winding and at times treacherous, but it was only a hundred and fifty miles from Komoro to Gifu, less than half the distance from Edo. Hidetada's brief, too, was straightforward enough. It was to drive all pockets of opposition before him into Mino, where they could deal with them jointly. The obvious reasoning behind this was to avoid being attacked in the rear by remnant pockets of resistance in Shinano, yet the chief objective remained Gifu castle.

Hidetada, however, was driven by the desire to make his mark even before the major battle, and the man he had singled out for conquest was Sanada Masayuki, the master of Ueda castle. Fifteen years earlier, in the summer of 1585, Ieyasu himself had attacked the castle with a force of seven thousand men, but after a siege of more than three months

The main gate of Komoro castle

he had withdrawn his troops without capturing a single stone. Hidetada knew that his father's forces had been repelled by no more two thousand of Masayuki's men. His spies informed him that, this time round, the warlord had raised roughly the same number, only a fraction of his own.

It was with some confidence, then, that the young commander set about to impress his father by avenging the ignominy the latter had suffered fifteen years earlier. Well before he had arrived at Komoro castle he had dispatched a number of letters to befriended chieftains in the region, summoning them to assist him in the pending siege of Ueda castle. On the day of his arrival at Komoro castle he sent a messenger to Ueda castle carrying a letter in which he ordered its owner to open the gates or face dire consequences. For two days the correspondence dragged on until it dawned on Hidetada that the shrewd Masayuki was biding his time, probably to await the arrival of reinforcements from allied warlords. Angered, he issued orders for his

Ueda castle

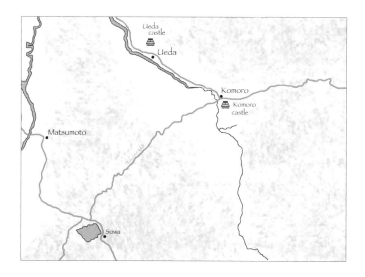

troops to encircle the castle. Yet, even as he moved his head-quarters to the vicinity of Someyadaira, a few miles east of the castle, it finally began to dawn on Hidetada that his plan had been too ambitious. Built on high grounds overlooking the Chikuma River, Ueda castle was indeed a formidable stronghold. Worse still, as the two days of stalling had proven, his enemy was a shrewd operator. He was also one of the most experienced strategists alive. In 1585 he had caused as many as fifteen hundred casualties among Ieyasu's troops while only sustaining a few dozen among his own men. To reduce Ueda castle was a daunting task, and to do it within the little time he had was perhaps impossible.

The situation was not helped by discord between his own generals. The old Honda Masanobu, one of Ieyasu's keenest strategists, who had been with him in Sakai on the night of the Honnō Rebellion, had advised Hidetada against the siege from the start, urging him to make haste to join his father in Mino as soon as possible. The young Makino Yasunari, who had a reputation to keep up as one of Ieyasu's most stalwart warrior generals, was strongly in favor of a direct assault on the castle, and regarded the old man's circumspection with near contempt. Yasunari's eagerness to fight must have communicated itself to his troops, for it was shortly into the siege that his troops charged the castle's main gate without Hidetada's orders, and one of the men who had set the charge in motion was none other than Mikogami Tenzen, Hidetada's personal fencing instructor.

Tadaaki had been appointed as *karita bugyō*, or chief of military police. This was an important post in feudal Japan, as the main duty of the *karita bugyō* was to keep undisciplined troops from foraging in local paddies and secretly harvesting rice to supplement their meager rations. It seems that Tenzen found it hard to adjust to his new role, for it was only a day into the siege that his warrior instincts got the better of him. The *Keichōki*, the records describing events during the years of Keichō (1596–1615) describe in vivid detail how:

> Early in the morning of October 12, two scouts, Yoda Hyōbu and Yamamoto Kiyoemon, left the castle and hid themselves behind a levy, some two hundred yards from the castle's main gate, which was guarded by the Sanada retainer Nezu Chōemon. They were followed by Saitō Sasuke, a foot soldier, who had dressed himself in

the garb of a *yamabushi* and began to call out his name and pedigree toward the enemy camp. As he did so he caught sight of Mikogami Tenzen and Tsuji Tarō no Suke from Makino Yasunari's camp, who came rushing toward him, the one after the other. When the unsuspecting men had reached the levy the two scouts suddenly jumped up and engaged them with their spears. The two, however, made their way up the levy and a pitched fight ensued. Then, five more men from the Tokugawa camp came running up and joined the fight.

Within moments the two Sanada retainers were overcome. Had the men been left to their own devices, the fighting would have ended there and then, but the hot-tempered Yasunari, spotting the skirmish from afar, ordered his cavalry of a hundred men to mount and make a charge on the main gate. This they did, but the gate guard, who had already brought his men into position, ordered his musketeers to fire. The volley caused a great number of casualties among

Main gate of Ueda castle

223

Yasunari's men, many of whom were thrown of their horses by the impact of the shot.

For three more days the siege dragged on in the same vein. Then, feeling that time was running out and egged on by the repeated admonitions from Honda Masanobu, Hidetada ordered his troops to return to Komoro castle and get ready to continue their march eastward along the Nakasendō. By the time they finally departed from Komoro, on October 17, his father had already reached Kiyosu castle to find that he was not there. Hidetada's failure to join his father in battle greatly damaged his reputation as a soldier and brought considerable shame on the house of Tokugawa. Ieyasu was rightfully incensed, but his response was lenient. He refused to see his son, but for only three days, causing some warlords to suspect that the shrewd strategist had conspired with his son to withhold his forces on purpose.

In a world where all things—good and bad—percolate downward through the ranks it was inevitable that those

Kiyosu castle, where Ieyasu awaited his son's arrival in vain

who were involved in the fiasco of the Ueda siege should feel the wrath of the Tokugawa. Nie Kamon, the commander who had led the ill-fated cavalry charge on the main gate of Ueda castle, was ordered to commit ritual suicide, and it was only through Makino Yasunari's personal intervention that Kamon escaped punishment. This, in turn, invited the wrath of Hidetada, who had Yasunari placed under house arrest, where he remained until 1604, when, upon the birth of Hidetada's second son he was pardoned in a nationwide amnesty. Tenzen and Tarō no Suke, too, were punished. Both were placed on parole, although a year later Tenzen was released and reinstalled as Hidetada's personal fencing instructor on a stipend of four hundred *koku*. Yet the ghost of Tenzen's role in the siege of Ueda castle continued to haunt him and his family members.

No such mishaps befell the house of Yagyū. Having fought bravely in the front lines among the troops of Tsutsui Sadatsugu, Munenori's stipend was raised to a thousand *koku*. In the nationwide redistribution of lands that followed in the wake of Sekigahara, all the Yagyū domains confiscated by Toyotomi Hidenaga in 1585 were returned to Yagyū Muneyoshi, who was raised to the rank of *hatamoto*. One year later the Yagyū domains were extended by another thousand *koku*, bringing the total amount of revenue that accrued to the Yagyū clan to more than four thousand *koku*. Munenori went on to serve two successive Tokugawa shoguns, first Hidetada, and then his son Iemitsu.

Over the following years, the Yagyū star continued to rise, reaching its apogee in 1632, when Munenori was raised

225

The Yagyū Yashiki, new abode of Yagyū Munenori

to the rank of *ōmetsuke*, or inspector general. By then the Yagyū domains had increased to well over ten thousand *koku*, making the Yagyū the first and only clan of swordsmen to reach the exalted position of daimyō.

It was at around this time that Munenori completed his work on a collection of writings that he named the *Heihō kadensho*, a record of all the hard lessons that his long and distinguished career had taught him. And it was in a chapter called *Katsujinken*, or "life-giving sword," that the daimyō reflected on the *mutōtori*, the technique that had so impressed Tokugawa Ieyasu and had put the Yagyū clan on the road to recovery from those bleak and depressing years:

> The aim of *mutō* is neither to take someone's sword, nor to cut someone down. If your enemy is intent on cutting you down, you should take his sword, but it should not be your aim from the start. The aim is to make the right judgment. You need to judge the right distance between you and the enemy to ensure his sword does

not strike you. If you are able to make the right judgment, you need not fear the strike of the enemy, and
when his sword does reach you, you will be able to esti-
mate the degree to which it does.

It has often been observed that what applies in art equally
applies in life, and so it was with the techniques of the Yagyū
Shinkage-ryū and the remarkable talents of those by whom
they had been developed. In both realms their unsurpassed
sense of judgment had given them the edge over their com-
petitors. Way back in 1567, at the fencing contest at the
Kōfuku monastery, Yagyū Muneyoshi had been humble
enough to recognize the superiority of Kamizumi
Nobutsuna's Shinkage-ryū and invite him to stay at Yagyū
castle. Later, when the province of Yamato descended into
anarchy, he had had the wisdom to go into hiding and impart
Nobutsuna's teachings to his son. In the end, it was in both
realms that they finally were able to reap the rewards they so
deserved. It had been Muneyoshi's superior fencing skills

A page from Munenori's
Heihō kadensho

227

that had given the Yagyū clan the opportunity to play a role in Tokugawa Ieyasu's grand campaign to unify the country, and it was Munenori's ability to make the right judgments that enabled them to build on their successes and attain a position of influence no other clan of swordsmen had, before or since. It was this position and their close association with the Tokugawa house, finally, that caused the Yagyū Shinkage school of fencing to eclipse the many other schools of fencing that had evolved in the course of the previous centuries and go on to become the most prestigious fencing school of the Edo period.

PRINCIPAL CHARACTERS IN THIS CHAPTER

Aisu Ikō:	Founder of the Kage school of fencing.
Akechi Mitsuhide:	Vassal of Oda Nobunaga, who turned against Nobunaga and assassinated him at the Honnō temple, and was later routed and killed by Toyotomi Hideyoshi at the village of Yamazaki.
Ashikaga Mochiuji:	*Kantō kubō* who fell out with his deputies and was forced to commit suicide.
Ashikaga Yoshiaki:	Fifteenth Muromachi shogun, who raised Kamiizumi Nobutsuna to the rank of Fourth-Level Warrior Follower.
Ashikaga Yoshiteru:	Thirteenth Muromachi shogun, who was assassinated by Matsunaga Hisahide.
Fukushima Masanori:	General of the eastern army, who led the second successful attack on Gifu castle and opened the Battle of Sekigahara.
Go-Daigo:	Emperor who sought to overthrow the Kamakura Bakufu and on whose behalf the Yagyū and Nakanobō clans fought during the Genkō Rebellion.
Honda Masanobu:	One of Tokugawa Hidetada's generals, who advised Hidetada against the siege of Ueda castle but to join his father in Mino.
Hōzōin In'ei:	Chief abbot of the Kōfuku monastery, who organized a fencing contest where he introduced Yagyū Muneyoshi to Kamiizumi Nobutsuna.
Ii Masanori:	Eastern commander who caused Fuku-shima Masanori to fire the first shots in anger in the Battle of Sekigahara

Ikeda Terumasa: General of the eastern army who led the first unsuccessful attack on Gifu castle.

Ishida Mitsunari: Warlord from Ōmi and leader of the western forces in the Battle of Sekigahara.

Kamiizumi Nobutsuna: Founder of the Shinkage school of fencing and teacher to Yagyū Muneyoshi during his stay at Yagyū castle and later during their period of hiding.

Katō Kiyomasa: General under whom Yagyū Kyūsaburō died in the defense of Ulsan castle during the second Korean campaign.

Kikkawa Hiroie: Western commander who was persuaded by Tokugawa Ieyasu to change sides and through whose actions Mōri Terumoto's forces failed to take part in the Battle of Sekigahara.

Kobayakawa Hideaki: Western warlord who initially joined Ishida Mitsunari in the siege of Fushimi castle, but helped Tokugawa Ieyasu into power by turning on Mitsunari in the Battle of Sekigahara.

Konishi Yukinaga: Western commander, whose forces eventually fled during the Battle of Sekigahara when those of Kobayakawa Hideaki turned against them.

Kuroda Nagamasa: Warlord from Buzen who introduced Yagyū Muneyoshi to Tokugawa Ieyasu and thereby revived the faltering fortunes of the Yagyū clan.

Makino Yasunari: One of Tokugawa Hidetada's generals who was in favor of laying siege of Ueda castle and led the failed cavalry charge.

Matsudaira Tadayoshi:	Eastern commander and fourth son of Tokugawa Ieyasu, who caused Fukushima Masanori to fire the first shots in anger in the Battle of Sekigahara.
Matsunaga Hisahide:	Warlord from Yamato and lord of Tamon castle.
Miyoshi Chōkei:	Warlord from Yamato who was succeeded as the leader of the Miyoshi clan by his senior counselor Matsunaga Hisahide.
Mōri Hidemoto:	Son of Mōri Terumoto who joined Ishida Mitsunari in the siege of Fushimi castle.
Mōri Terumoto:	Member of the Council of Five Regents who failed to chose sides in the Battle of Sekigahara.
Oda Hidenobu:	Grandson of Oda Nobunaga, who resisted Tokugawa Ieyasu's forces from Gifu castle but was eventually forced to surrender.
Oda Nobunaga:	Warlord from Owari, and the first of Japan's three great unifiers.
Ōtani Yoshitsugu:	Western commander, whose forces eventually fled during the Battle of Sekigahara when those of Kobayakawa Hideaki turned against them.
Sakuma Nobumori:	One of Oda Nobunaga's generals, who led the campaign of 1568 to subdue Yamato and drove out the Miyoshi.
Sanada Masayuki:	Lord of Ueda castle, who managed to hold out against the forces of Tokugawa Hidetada and thereby caused the latter to fail to arrive in Ōmi in time to join his father in the Battle of Sekigahara.

Shimazu Toyohisa:	Western commander whose failure to come to the rescue of the Konishi and Ukita troops led to the defeat of the western forces in the Battle of Sekigahara.
Takeda Shingen:	Warlord from Kai and main rival of Hōjō Ujitsuna.
Takeuchi Hidekatsu:	Chief commander of Matsunaga Hisahide, who pressured the Yagyū clan to fight against the forces of Tsutsui Junkei.
Tokugawa Hidetada:	Son of Tokugawa Ieyasu, who failed to join his father in the Battle of Sekigahara by laying siege of Ueda castle in Shinano.
Tokugawa Ieyasu:	Warlord from Mikawa, and the third of Japan's three great unifiers.
Torii Mototada:	Warden of Fushimi castle who laid down his life in its defense against Ishida Mitsunari's forces.
Toyotomi Hidenaga:	Toyotomi Hideyoshi's stepbrother, who replaced Tsutsui Sadatsugu as the governor of Yamato and became the new lord of Kōriyama castle.
Toyotomi Hidetsugu:	Nephew and adoptive heir to Toyotomi Hideyoshi, who fell out of grace with his adoptive father and was eventually forced to commit suicide.
Toyotomi Hideyoshi:	Warlord from Owari, and the second of Japan's three great unifiers.
Tsutsui Junkei:	Warrior from Yamato who sought to restore the fortunes of his clan by overthrowing their archrival, Matsunaga Hisahide.
Tsutsui Junsei:	Uncle and patron of Tsutsui Junkei.

Tsutsui Sadatsugu:	Adoptive son and successor to Tsutsui Junkei, who was forced by Toyotomi Hideyoshi to move to the neighboring province of Iga from where he began the construction of Ueno castle and from where he and Yagyū Munenori later rode into battle to join Tokugawa Ieyasu in the Battle of Sekigahara.
Uesugi Kagekatsu:	Member of the Council of Five Regents, whose rebellion gave Tokugawa Ieyasu the chance to create the conditions for Ishida Mitsunari's revolt.
Uesugi Kenshin:	Warlord from Echigo and rival of Hōjō Ujitsuna who came to the rescue of Satomi Yoshitaka.
Ukita Hideie:	Western commander, who joined Ishida Mitsunari in the siege of Fushimi castle, but whose forces fled during the Battle of Sekigahara when those of Kobayakawa Hideaki turned against them.
Yagyū Ieyoshi:	Grandfather of Yagyū Munenori.
Yagyū Kyūsaburō:	Son of Yagyū Yoshikatsu who died in the defense of Ulsan castle during the Korean campaign.
Yagyū Muneaki:	Fourth oldest brother of Yagyū Munenori, who entered the service of the Kyushu warlord Kobayakawa Hideaki.
Yagyū Munetaka:	Third oldest brother of Yagyū Munenori, who took the tonsure and assumed the name of Tokusai.
Yagyū Muneyoshi:	Father of Yagyū Munenori and founder of the Yagyū Shinkage school of fencing.

Yagyū Nagayoshi: Yagyū Munenori's distant ancestor, who fought on behalf of Emperor Go-Daigo during the Genkō Rebellion.

Yagyū Yoshihide: Second oldest brother of Yagyū Munenori, who took the tonsure and assumed the name of Kyūsai.

Yagyu Yoshikatsu: Oldest brother of Yagyū Munenori, who was wounded in Nara during a battle between the forces of Matsunaga Hisahide and Tsutsui Junkei.

Yagyū Yoshitaka: Brother of Yagyū Nagayoshi, who entered the service of Emperor Go-Daigo.

Yodogimi: Toyotomi Hideyoshi's mistress, who bore his second son and heir, Hideyori.

OLD PROVINCES

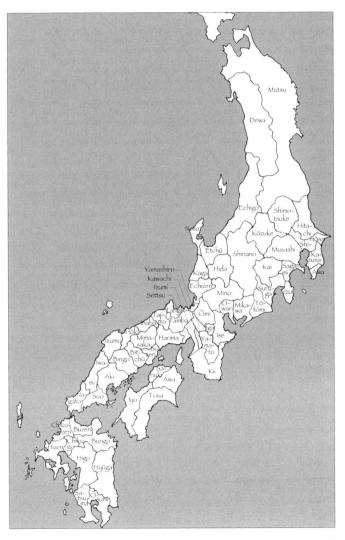

OLD PROVINCES AND THEIR MODERN EQUIVALENTS

Aki:	Hiroshima	Kawachi:	Osaka
Awa:	Tokushima	Kazusa:	Chiba
Bingo:	Hiroshima	Kii:	Wakayama
Bitchū:	Okayama	Kōzuke:	Gunma
Bizen:	Okayama	Mikawa:	Aichi
Bungo:	Ōita	Mimasaka:	Okayama
Buzen:	Fukuoka	Mino:	Gifu
Chikugo:	Fukuoka	Musashi:	Saitama and Tokyo
Chikuzen:	Fukuoka	Mutsu:	Aomori
Dewa:	Yamagata, Akita	Nagato:	Yamaguchi
Echigo:	Niigata	Noto:	Ishikawa
Echizen:	Fukui	Ōmi:	Shiga
Etchū:	Fukuyama	Ōsumi:	Kagoshima
Harima:	Hyōgo	Owari:	Aichi
Hida:	Gifu	Sagami:	Kanagawa
Higo:	Kumamoto	Sanuki:	Kagawa
Hitachi:	Ibaraki	Satsuma:	Kagoshima
Hizen:	Nagasaki	Settsu:	Osaka
Hōki:	Tottori	Shimōsa:	Chiba
Hyūga:	Miyazaki	Shinano:	Nagano
Iga:	Mie	Suō:	Yamaguchi
Inaba:	Tottori	Suruga:	Shizuoka
Ise:	Mie	Tajima:	Hyōgo
Iwami:	Shimane	Tamba:	Kyoto
Iyo:	Ehime	Tango:	Kyoto
Izu:	Shizuoka	Tosa:	Kōchi
Izumi:	Osaka	Tōtōmi:	Shizuoka
Izumo:	Shimane	Wakasa:	Fukui
Kaga:	Ishikawa	Yamashiro:	Kyoto
Kai:	Yamanashi	Yamato:	Nara

CASTLES, SHRINES, AND TEMPLES

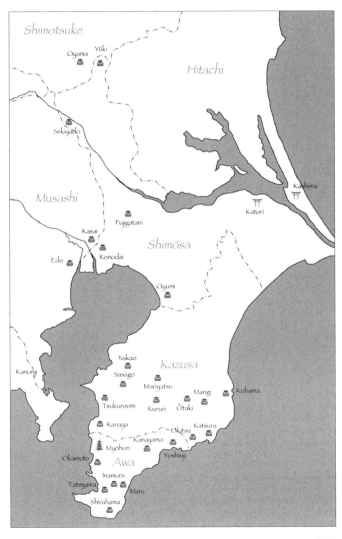

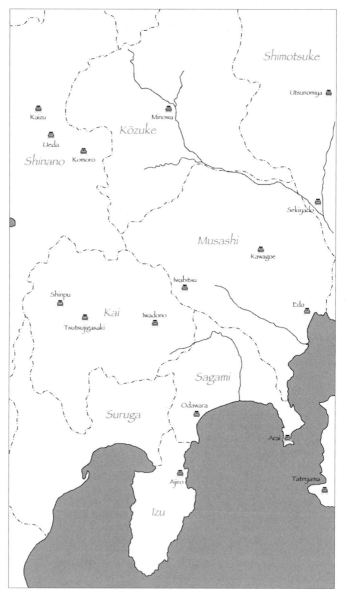

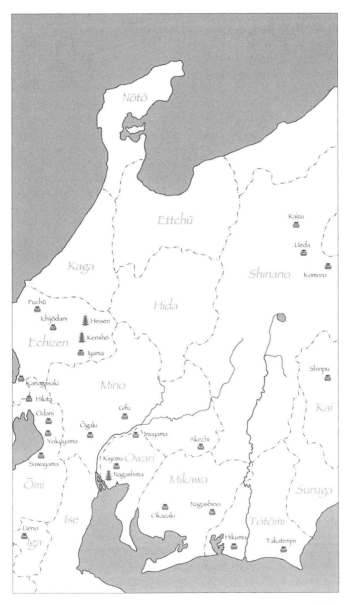

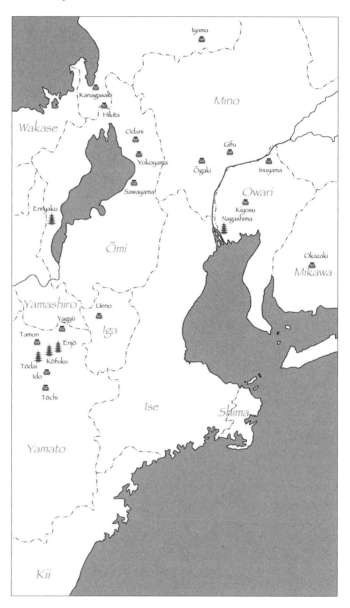

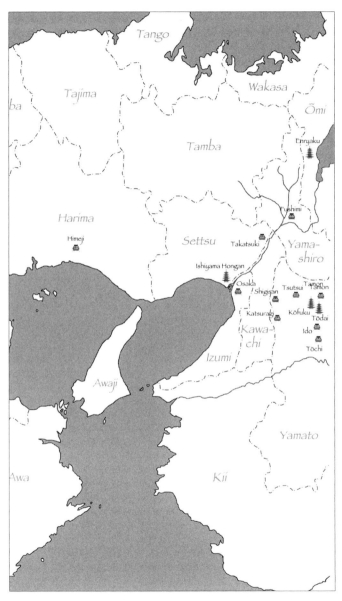

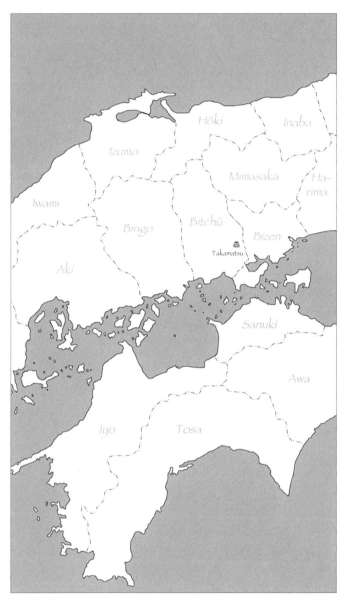

HISTORICAL PERIODS

JAPAN

Nara	710–94
Heian	794–1185
Kamakura	1185–1333
Muromachi	1333–1568
Momoyama	1568–1600
Tokugawa	1600–1868

CHINA

Han	202 BC–AD 220
Three Kingdoms	221–65
Six Dynasties	265–581
Sui	581–618
Tang	618–906
Five Dynasties	907–60
Northern Song	960–1127
Southern Song	1127–1279
Yuan	1271–1368
Ming	1368–1644
Qing	1644–1911

PERIODS OF MILITARY RULE

Kamakura Bakufu	1185–1333
Muromachi Bakufu (Ashikaga Bakufu)	1333–1568
Edo Bakufu (Tokugawa Bakufu)	1603–1867

BATTLES AND REBELLIONS

BATTLES

Battle of Inukake	1534
Battles of Konodai:	1538, 64
Battles of Kawanakajima	1553–61
Battle of Okehazama	1560
Battle of Mt. Mifune	1567
Battles of Sekiyado	1565–74
Battle of Ane River	1570
Battle of Mikatagahara	1572
Battle of Nagashima	1574
Battle of Nagashino	1575
Battle of Komakiyama	1584
Battle of Nagakute	1584
Battle of Odawara castle	1590
Battle of Sekigahara:	1600

REBELLIONS

Jinshin Rebellion	672
Hōgen Rebellion:	1156
Heiji Rebellion:	1159
Jōkyū Rebellion	1221
Genkō Rebellion	1331
Honnō Rebellion	1582

GLOSSARY

ashigaru:	Type of footsoldier that came into its own during the Ōnin War, but were organized into disciplined regiments by Oda nobunaga.
bokken:	Practice sword made of tropical hardwood.
bunbu ryōdō:	The dual way of learning and fighting.
deshi:	Disciple.
dōjō:	Hall with a smooth wooden floor or covered with mats for the practice of martial arts.
fudai daimyō:	Vassal daimyō.
gekokujō:	Term used to describe the overthrow of higher military classes by the lower.
go-bugyō:	Council of (five) Commissioners.
go-tairō:	Council of (five) Regents.
hakama:	A trousered skirt, worn by the samurai.
honmaru:	The innermost keep of a castle.
ichiban kubi:	The first enemy head to be taken in battle.
inka:	Certificate of an apprentice's maturity in training.
kanpaku:	Regent.
kanbe:	Families attached to a shrine.
kenchi:	Land survey.
kiai:	Fearsome cry uttered by a warrior to release his powers and intimidate his opponent.
koku:	Medieval unit of measurement, approximately 180 liters. One *koku* was considered the quantity of rice required to sustain one person for one year.
mokuroku:	Written inventory of the techniques and tenets of a school of swordsmanship.
mukaijō:	Makeshift stronghold built facing existing strongholds to isolated it from others.

musha shugyō:	Literally, "warrior training," but in the context of *budō*, the practice of ascetic self-discipline that goes back to the ancient traditions of the mysterious *yamabushi*, or mountain monks.
mutōtori:	Disarming one's opponent without the use of one's sword.
naginata:	Pole sword.
ochimusha:	Warriors who as a result of their defeat were reliant on the hospitality and protection of others.
okugi:	Innermost secrets of an art or craft.
ōmetsuke:	Inspector general.
rōnin:	Masterless samurai.
senjū:	The martial art of divination.
shihan:	Personal fencing instructor.
sōhei:	Warrior monks of the great Buddhist temples.
sōjutsu:	Art of fighting with a halberd.
taikō:	Retired regent.
taikō kenchi:	The nationwide land surveys conducted by Toyotomi Hideyoshi between 1582 and 1598.
taitō:	Longsword.
taryū shiai:	Literally, "contest of different schools," used to refer to a duel between two swordsmen.
tenka fubu:	Rule the whole country by force.
wakō:	Japanese pirates who pillaged the coasts of China and Korea during the middle ages.
yagura:	(Castle) turret or defensive scaffolding.
yamabushi:	Reclusive mountain monks of the Japanese Alps, who practiced austerities in the harsh environment of the mountains in order to attain holy or super-human powers.
yari:	Spear or lance.
zōei bugyō:	Construction magistrates.

BIBLIOGRAPHY

ENGLISH SOURCES

Friday, Karl F. *Hired Swords*, 1992.

Mason, R. H. P., and J. G. Caiger. *A History of Japan*. Tokyo, 1972.

Mass, Jeffrey P. *The Origins of Japan's Medieval World*, 1997.

Sansom, George. *A History of Japan*. Vols. 1–3. Tokyo, 1963.

Sato Hiroaki. *Legends of the Samurai*. New York, 1995.

Turnbull, S. R. *The Samurai*. New York, 1977.

——— . *Warriors of Japan*. Honolulu, 1994.

JAPANESE SOURCES

Abe Takeshi, *Sengoku jinmei jiten*, Tokyo, 1990.

Fukuda Akira. *Chūsei katarimono bungei*. Tokyo, 1981.

Hioki Shōichi. *Nihon sōhei kenkyū*. Tokyo, 1972.

Hirotani Yūtarō. *Nihon kendō shiryō*. Tokyo, 1943.

Imamura Yoshio. *Shiryō Yagyū shinkageryū*. Vols. 1–2. Tokyo, 1995.

——— . *Yamato Yagyū ichizoku*. Tokyo, 1974.

Kaionji Chōgorō. *Bushō retsuden*. Vols. 1–6. Tokyo, 1965.

Kitagawa Hiroshi. *Gunkimono no keifu*. Kyoto, 1985.

Kojima Hidehiro, *Kengō densetsu*, Tokyo, 1997.

—. *Sugao no kengōtachi*. Tokyo, 1998.

Kuwata Tadachika. *Chosaku-shū*. Vols. 1–10. Tokyo. 1980.

——— . *Nihon no kengō*. Vols. 1–5. Tokyo, 1984.

Maki Hidehiko. *Kengō zenshi*. Tokyo, 2003.

Matsumura Hiroshi. *Rekishi monogatari*. Tokyo, 1979.

Mizuno Yasuo. *Sengoku daimyō Asakurashi to Ichijōdani*. Tokyo, 2002.

Nagazumi Yasuaki. *Gunki monogatari no sekai*. Tokyo, 1978.

Nakajima Michiko. *Yagyū Sekishūsai Muneyoshi*. Tokyo, 2003.

Nakamura Akira. *Shinkage-ryū Kamiizumi Nobutsuna*. Tokyo, 2004.

Nanjō Norio. *Nihon no meijō, kojō jiten*. Tokyo, 1997.

Naoki Sukeyama, *Nihon kengō retsuden*, 1983.

Nikki Ken'ichi. *Gassen no butai-ura*. Tokyo, 1976.

Nishigaya Yasuhiro, *Sengoku daimyō jōkaku jiten*, Tokyo, 1999.

Ōmori Nobumasa. *Bujutsu densho no kenkyū*. Tokyo, 1991.

Owada Tetsuo. *Toyotomi Hideyoshi*. Tokyo, 1985.

Sennohara Yasukata. *Bōsō Satomi suigun no kenkyū*. Tokyo, 1997.

——. *Kokufudai no gassen*. Tokyo, 1977.

——. *Shinpen Bōsō sengoku-shi*, Tokyo, 2000.

Sugimoto Keizaburō. *Gunki monogatari no sekai*. Tokyo, 1985.

Sukeyama Naoki. *Nihon kengō retsuden*. Tokyo, 1983.

Takahashi Tomio. *Bushidō no rekishi*. Vols. 1–3. Tokyo, 1986.

Takano Samirō. *Kendō*. Tokyo, 1915.

Takemitsu Makoto. *Gassen no Nihon chizu*. Tokyo, 2003.

Taniguchi Katsuhiro. *Nobunaga no shineitai*. Tokyo, 1998.

Tokunaga Shinichirō. *Yagyū Munenori*, Tokyo, 1978.

Watatani Kiyoshi. *Nihon gassen zenshū*. Vols. 1–6, Tokyo, 1990.

——. *Nihon kengō no hyaku sen*. Tokyo, 1990.

Yasuda Motohisa. *Kamakura, Muromachi jinmei jiten*. Tokyo, 1990.

Yokoi Kiyoshi. *Chūsei wo ikita hitobito*. Kyoto, 1981.

INDEX

Bold type indicates a page with an illustration

Floating World Editions publishes books that contribute to a deeper understanding of Asian cultures. Editorial supervision: Ray Furse. Book and cover design: William de Lange. Maps and charts: John de Lange. Production supervision: Bill Rose. Printing and binding: Malloy Incorporated. The typefaces used are Hoefler and Papyrus.